D1462383

Real Dream Teams

Seven Practices Used by World-Class Team Leaders to Achieve Extraordinary Results

Real Dream Teams

Seven Practices Used by World-Class Team Leaders to Achieve Extraordinary Results

Bob Fisher & Bo Thomas

S_L^t

ST. LUCIE PRESS

A CRC Press Company
Boca Raton   London   New York   Washington, D.C.

Library of Congress Cataloging-in-Publication Data
Catalog record is available from the Library of Congress

Visit the CRC Press Web site at www.crcpress.com

© 1996 by CRC Press
St Lucie Press is an imprint of CRC Press

No claim to original U S Government works
International Standard Book Number 1-57444-006-3
Printed in the United States of America   8 9 0
Printed on acid-free paper

To

Our parents

who taught us teams

and

Our families

Who are our best real dream teams:

Judy, Kelly,	Rubye Lynn
Rob, Jennifer,	Elizabeth,
Neil, and Josh	and Stephanie

with a special dedication to

Paul Whitley

who inspired our efforts

TABLE OF CONTENTS

ACKNOWLEDGMENTS

As with any meaningful effort in today's complex, highly interdependent world, the completion of this book required the support and cooperation of a large number of people.

The first acknowledgment goes to Becky Cowling, who, through the years involved in this project, was always cooperative, supportive, and competent in her role as informal editor. Other Henderson people who enabled this work are David Thomson, who provided input on the first draft of the manuscript; the Henderson State University Faculty Research Committee, who provided partial funding for gathering information; Pam Antonacci, who assisted with the final stages of research; and Joe Clark, Bob's boss, who let him keep his job in spite of the time and travel demands required to make this project successful. We are both indebted to numerous students who have encouraged and challenged us over the years.

We also want to acknowledge two types of "door openers." The first type includes people who helped us to arrange the interviews with our real dream team leaders. These people were Dr. Lee Kuyper at Burroughs Wellcome, Gwen Snow at Ford, Archie Schaffer and Cleta Selman at Tyson, Col. Eddie and Kay Buffington for the Brady interview, as well as Dr. Fred Gordy and Jerry Adams, who helped arrange the Holtz and Peale interviews, respectively.

The second type of "door opener" includes people who have invited us into their organizations as consultants and given us the opportunity to develop a team process that enables people to work together more effectively. These people include, but are not limited to, Fran Shove and Wayne Ready at Kimberly-Clark; Bob Francour at Best Foods; Steve Seitz at Post Cereals; Mike Means at Arkla; Phil Sutphin, Bill Hubbard, and Collins Andrews at Alltel Information Services; Milt Honea at Noram; Don Bailey at the City of Fayetteville; Pat Sweeden at Maybelline; Jerry Newman, Paul Webb, and Dick Reedy at Reynolds; and Paul Whitley at Tyson Foods, along with at least one hundred others who have made major contributions to our thinking and work.

A special thank you to Kelly Fisher for reading the manuscript and creating the cover illustration to reflect her vision of real dream teams.

INTRODUCTION

"Do you believe in miracles?" shouted Al Michaels to a worldwide television audience captivated and thrilled by what they were witnessing. As the final seconds ticked away, Herb Brooks' "Boys of Winter" achieved an incredible victory against the powerful Soviet Union ice hockey team in the 1980 Olympics on their way to bringing home the gold for the United States. The achievement was so spectacular and so improbable that the word "miracle" indeed captured the moment. It was like a dream come true—a "*real* dream team." Outstanding teamwork, cohesiveness, and bone-deep dedication to a mission defeated the superior individual talent of the Soviet team.

Dream teams are exciting. They capture our imagination. The phrase "dream team" is often used to describe a group of people working together for a common objective who achieve extraordinary success. The achievement seems so spectacular that it's as if we are dreaming.

When we ask people to tell us what first comes to mind when they hear the phrase "dream team," more often than not they mention the 1992 U.S. Olympic basketball team. With an all-star cast, which included professional players such as Michael Jordan, Charles Barkley, and Scottie Pippen, among others, the U.S. team totally dominated their opponents in winning the Gold Medal.

Using the phrase "dream team" to describe this group is not quite accurate. They didn't really win because of spectacular teamwork. It was the individual talent of each player that was spectacular; the teamwork was just okay. We have also heard the phrase used to refer to the "Hollywood dream team" of Steven Spielberg, Jeffrey Katzenberg, and David Geffen who are forming a new studio, or even the O.J. Simpson defense lawyers.

It would be more accurate to use the phrase "dream *talent*" to describe these all-stars. Because the phrase "dream team" has often been misused in this way, we want to make it clear that our focus is on "*real* dream teams," like the 1980 U.S. hockey team—teams that achieve extraordinary results through synergistic group dynamics.

When a real dream team experience occurs, it seems magical. We have all had our moments—those times when we have been a part of an extraordinary team effort that succeeded beyond our wildest dreams. These experiences are characterized by a high level of motivation that brings out the best in us, and they just feel good! For most of us, these experiences are all too rare. They seem to occur almost randomly or when we just get lucky.

The prescription for how to participate in or lead teams to become dream teams seems illusive. But what if we could capture the conditions or practices that maximize best team efforts? What if those fleeting moments when we experience our best in personal or professional relationships could be enhanced? What if those dreams weren't out of reach because we discovered a process that capitalized on those inherent motivational qualities that allow us to succeed, do our best, and work/live cooperatively with others.

There is such a process that allows dreams to create reality. A process exists to encourage the dream, the sharing of the dream, and the collective ownership of the dream. This is a process that values dreaming and visioning as a first priority, recognizing that plans and actions can be meaningful and powerful only if they follow the dream.

While creating dream teams is certainly not easy, all of us are capable of becoming more effective team leaders and team members. It is not a magical process. Creating a structure and process for achieving this increased effectiveness is what this book is all about. The creation of this structure will involve utilizing your own dream team experiences and the experiences of people we have come to know through our team-building sessions, as well as the experiences of what we will refer to throughout this book as twelve "dream team leaders." These twelve individuals are leaders of dream teams that have been awarded national championships, a Nobel Prize, a Medal of Honor, a best-in-industry award, and other forms of recognition of top levels of achievement.

Why Teams?

Today's world cries out for a different, more collaborative, less traditional response to the problems we face. Consider the need for effective leadership and followership that exists in just the few following examples of basic societal roles.

Parents—Like it or not, the role of parent has shifted radically in the past twenty years. Neither Ward and June Cleaver nor Ozzie and Harriet Nelson are the common role models for today's family. But the need remains for parent(s) to build deep and meaningful relationships with their children as they fulfill the parental role of nurturing, instilling key values, and teaching successful patterns of behavior.

Couples—People want to know how to live meaningfully and work cooperatively and supportively in building a true partnership.

Managers and supervisors—Work leaders in all types of organizations (business, government, military, health care, etc.) want to know how to organize work efforts and empower people so they will be able to compete effectively.

Community leaders and volunteers—There is a need to restore a true sense of community or support for the common good of what is becoming an increasingly diverse group of people who live in close proximity to one another.

Teachers—Many teachers are beginning to utilize students as significant learning resources, while at the same time teaching students patterns of cooperative behavior that will prepare them to be successful in a wide range of roles.

The traditional patterns of behavior that have accompanied these and other important roles in our society have been based on authority, position, status, hierarchy, rank, control, and power. These responses seemed to work reasonably well for many years, but not anymore. The world is constantly changing, but in recent years the changes in society and technology that seemed to be evolutionary in the past have become increasingly revolutionary. If we truly live in a "new environment," then it makes sense that we must develop new behavioral responses to that new environment.

The New Environment

Many of us have grown weary of the overuse of "new" to describe a product, service, or idea. But we're going to risk irritating you by referring to today's socio-technical environment as different enough to be classified as "new."

At the beginning of *The Wizard of Oz*, young Dorothy is suddenly transported from her home in Kansas to a radically different place where almost everything seems new to her and her little dog Toto. As many of us stop and look around at our environment today, we may feel a lot like Dorothy as she says with great wonder and some fear, "Toto, I have a feeling we're not in Kansas anymore!"

If we're not in Kansas anymore, then where are we and what characterizes this "Land of Oz" in which we find ourselves? We can thrive in our new "Land of Oz" if we recognize and accept the realities that shape our new world and learn to face it together. Five major forces are shaping this new environment, and they can best be faced with team responses.

Competitiveness

The fight for scarce resources continues to intensify as more and more people, informed by a broader distribution of knowledge, compete for everything from jobs and business markets to acceptance into prestigious universities. (When one of our children was a seventh grader, she said the reason she was joining a certain school club was so she could "build her resume for college!") Because of its very nature, competition forces people to either "get with it" and get into the game or be left behind.

We once heard Tom Peters, the management author and prophet, tell of a conversation he had several years ago with a crusty, traditional, fifty-seven-year-old executive at a break during one of his speaking engagements. Peters was discussing the book *In Search of Excellence*, which he and Bob Waterman authored. The book outlines some fundamental changes in business practices that the authors believe are required if the United States is to be successful in an increasingly competitive world.

The man told Tom Peters, "I want you to know that

I bought your book." "That's great!" Peters replied. "I didn't like it much though," the man continued, "but I still came to hear you speak today." "I'm glad you did," Peters responded politely. The man continued the awkward conversation by saying, "I don't like what I'm hearing you say today either." Then, after a thoughtful pause, the man concluded, "but I don't think that we've got any choice!" No force has changed the environment in which we live more than competition, and we have limited choices as to whether or not we will respond.

We also see misguided, dysfunctional competitiveness in a wide range of situations. We see family members, co-workers, and a variety of other teammates competing with each other rather than working together cooperatively toward a common mission. One of the most important things a team can do is spend whatever time is necessary to clearly answer the question, "Who is the competition?" It is not that unusual to discover we are competing with people who are on our team. When that happens, the classic "Pogo" cartoon comes to mind: "We have met the enemy and he is us!"

Self-Centeredness

During the 1980s, very little effort was made to disguise, much less repress, this basic characteristic of human nature. The attitude of that decade was appropriately tagged the "me generation." From the athletic field to Wall Street, the message could not have been any clearer: "If you don't take care of yourself, then nobody will." "Look out for number one." "Do unto others before they have a chance to do unto you." Team-based values such as caring for and supporting others, searching for win–win solutions rather than seeing every problem as a win–lose confrontation, and respecting the inherent value and worth of all people were pretty much out of step in the 1980s.

High Expectations

The focus on achieving high levels of quality in business, school, government, and other organizations/institutions has been absolutely necessary and most healthy. But *some* of the expectations that the total quality management philosophy has generated seem unrealistic to some people and thus raise their stress levels. Marriage partners are expecting more of each other than ever before. As roles change, new functions are added to roles, but very few old functions are dropped. Some husbands even believed the woman in a 1980s commercial who said, "I can bring home the bacon, fry it up in a pan, and never, ever let you forget you're a man!" Somehow the message that more teamwork is necessary on the home front when both partners are working was missed.

Children seem to expect parents to do it all—earn enormous amounts of money to support them in a comfortable lifestyle and always be there when they want to talk. And when they talk, they expect to be able to solve any problem in an hour or less, just like the families they see on television. Students seem to expect teachers to be as much fun as professional entertainers. Customer expectations for rapid responses and quality services and products are overwhelming the marketplace. Team approaches are a big part of the solution to addressing and achieving these higher expectations.

Accelerating Change

While it is natural and understandable for people to resist change, the environment of today and tomorrow will be most rewarding to those who embrace and master the change process. The reality of accelerating change has been clearly addressed in the past few years by authors such as Toffler (*Future Shock* and *The Third Wave*), Kanter (*The Change Masters*), Naisbitt (*Megatrends*), Naisbitt and

Aburdene (*Re-Inventing the Corporation*), Peters (*Thriving on Chaos*), Tichy and Sherman (*Control Your Own Destiny or Someone Else Will*), and numerous others.

We recently heard someone in a rapidly growing high-tech organization remark, "When things get back to normal around here, then I'll be able to regain control." We have some bad news for this person: things will never be "normal" again! The rate of change is certainly not going to slow; in fact, all indications are that it will continue to accelerate. The people who will be most successful in this environment will be those who master change and thrive on chaos. Those who choose to resist the need to change should be confronted with the question asked by MIT economist Dr. Lester Thurow:

> We've only got two choices in this competitive environment:
>
> 1. We can lose
>
> or
>
> 2. We can change.
>
> Which do you choose?

Well, we're certainly not losers. After checking to make certain there is no third choice, we were forced to join the previously referred to crusty, traditional, fifty-seven-year-old who said, "I don't think we've got any choice." We must be willing to work at change, even if it means finding new ways of living together.

Increased Interdependence

The effective functioning of society is rapidly becoming increasingly complex and interdependent. The American mentality of independent thought and independent action has led us to create individual heroes, even when team efforts were involved. Independence continues to be strongly valued in the United States. Ask a typical American fifth grader how he or she would go about completing a job that must be done. The typical reply will probably be something like, "You have to do it yourself!" In many Eastern countries, the reply would be very different, more along the lines of "I will ask my classmates to help me and then we can do it!"

The concept of "chaos theory" is beginning to gain the attention of more people as it helps us to think differently about the interrelatedness of our existence. In her address to the American Council of Education Women President's Summit, Barbara Mossberg summarized some key points about chaos theory:

> When we compare the ways that things become different, no matter what these things are (galaxies, cell growth, falling water, lightning, populations), we see a pattern in how movement occurs and is manifested, a pattern that shows the interconnectedness of things of different scale, size, kind, and form in the universe. But these relationships are only apparent when we compare them. Rather than be understood as the opposite of order, "chaos theory" redefines order to include the patterns and interconnections that exist but only become perceptible when we see them in the context of the whole. Thus "chaos theory" is the science of "wholeness" and comprehensive relatedness, and by definition, the philosophy of diversity and unity. Since it shows the fundamental relationship of order and chaos, unity and diversity, it provides a new perspective on issues confronting us. We can say that this is a "global" perspective that sees patterns and connections and above all, knows that order and relatedness exist, even if they are not immediately apparent.

Interrelatedness is really not a new idea. "Ask not for whom the bell tolls, it tolls for thee," wrote John Donne many years ago in his famous sermon "No Man Is an

Island." "For whom the bell tolls" expresses at the deepest level what we believe about teams. At one level, the concept of teams is very simple and straightforward yet profound: we need each other. In today's sophisticated, highly complex world, it is most unlikely that any of us will accomplish anything of significance without the help of a lot of other people. At another level, implementing teamwork becomes very complex because of the concept of self-interest which lies at the heart of human nature. The obvious need for teamwork we logically recognize is countered by the "gut level" emotional reaction that narrowly seeks the selfish goals of the individual.

"For whom the bell tolls" is the ultimate expression of humankind's ironic lack of understanding of our interconnectedness and interdependence. When someone dies, we are all diminished. Sometimes the loss is clear, especially when we lose someone very close to us or when someone who has made a great contribution to society dies (Norman Vincent Peale, Edwards Deming, or Eleanor Roosevelt). However, when an old, homeless, nameless man dies, our linkage, interdependence, and loss are not as clear. But we contend, along with John Donne, that when the bell tolls for this person, it also tolls for you and me because a part of us and our potential has been diminished.

This rather serious, philosophical discussion is not intended to discourage you; rather, it is intended to communicate the seriousness, importance, and potential of teams. Besides, if this means we are to grieve the loss of every human, then it also means we are to celebrate with great joy the potential represented by the birth of every child!

The magnificent opening scene to the Disney classic *The Lion King* captures the spirit of our interconnectedness in a stunning fashion. As the song "The Circle of Life" is performed, the wise old baboon named Rafiki presents the newborn cub Simba to the world in a truly inspiring ceremony that is all about the processes that link every living creature to one another.

Teams Tackle The New Environment

To achieve success in this challenging new environment will require the best efforts of everyone. A survey a few years ago reported that only about 20 percent of American workers described their daily work effort as being their best. Imagine that! How many games do you think an athletic team in a competitive environment could expect to win if only 20 percent of its team members were willing to give their best effort? The survey went on to report an even more perplexing finding: more than 80 percent of those surveyed said they were willing and able to make a significantly greater contribution to their organization *if* they could be shown a reason for putting forth the additional effort and *if* their increased effort would make a difference.

Teams are the most natural and fundamental building blocks of society. Whether we are talking about families, communities, business organizations, churches or synagogues, or a host of other collective efforts, the strategy for energizing the best efforts of everybody in a cooperative environment must be driven by teamwork. A team mentality is required to generate the commitment, responsiveness, flexibility, and acceptance of responsibility that are necessary to thrive in the new environment.

The teamwork vehicle is readily available and can build on existing resources. It requires no new technology, equipment, or capital expenditure and new people. What teamwork does require is what often amounts to a considerably different way of thinking. We talked with Donald Petersen, former CEO of Ford Motor Company, just one month before his retirement from that position. Near the conclusion of the interview, we asked him, "What is your legacy to Ford Motor Company—what are you most proud of?" We expected him to name a particular automobile that was developed under his leadership, such as the Lincoln Town Car, or to point to the "Team Taurus" project. After a thoughtful pause, Petersen responded:

> The thing I'm most proud of, the thing that I hope will live in this company long after I'm gone, my greatest hope of a lasting contribution is that the people of Ford Motor Company will work together differently than they did when I first assumed leadership—they will work as a team.

For people to successfully work together in the new environment, many of them must change their individual attitudes and behaviors, and organizational systems must change.

"The Goose Story" (author unknown) presents a very straightforward case for the power of teams:

> Next fall when you see geese heading south for the winter, flying along in a "V" formation, you might be interested to know why they fly that way.
>
> As each bird flaps its wings, it creates an uplift for the bird immediately following. By flying in a "V" formation, the whole flock adds at least 71% greater flying range than if each bird flew on its own. **People who share common direction and sense of community can get where they are going quicker and easier, because they are traveling on the thrusts of one another.**
>
> When a goose falls out of formation, it suddenly feels the drag and resistance of trying to go it alone, and quickly returns to formation to take advantage of the lifting power. **If we have sense like a goose, we will stay in formation with those who are headed the same way we are going.**
>
> When the lead goose gets tired, he rotates back in the wing and another goose flies point. **It pays to take turns doing hard jobs.**

The geese honk from behind to encourage those up front to keep up their speed. **An encouraging word goes a long way.**

Finally, when a goose gets sick or is wounded and falls out, two geese fall out of formation and follow him down to help and protect him. They stay with him until he is either able to fly or until he is dead, and they then launch out on their own or with another formation. **If we have the sense of a goose, we will stand by each other like that.**

Unfortunately, very bright and sensible people are distracted from the basics of teamwork by culture and systems that reward individuality at the expense of the collective good.

Over The Wall

It's the first day of an outdoor team-building session where the team is presented with several novel challenges. The team members have just emerged from the woods into a small clearing to face a fourteen-foot-high wall. Their task is to scale the wall without using any tools (ladders, ropes, etc.) except each other, and they must not leave any team member behind. To ease your suspense, we'll tell you that the team made it over the wall in less than ten minutes. In fact, every team we've taken through this experience has been successful, even though this is a genuinely difficult task and there is no easy trick to it.

The first relevant point is not that the team got over the wall, but rather that the first impulse of over 80 percent of the people who face this challenge is, "We can't do it—it's impossible." Four out of five people silently say no, which is understandable because it seems impossible.

The second relevant point is that teams invariably conquer this impossible task. They do it because it is the expectation of the day and because they know they are there to meet challenges, solve problems, and face these and other "walls" as a team. We have seen groups demonstrate their best teamwork at these walls; the tougher the challenge, the better the teamwork. Why do these really tough situations produce such extraordinary teamwork? The reason is that it becomes blatantly obvious that nobody can be successful alone; in other words, people can't overcome huge challenges unless they stick together. The challenging walls of the new environment can only be scaled with the best of everybody.

Best Team Experience

We began our research on how to create and maintain excellence in teamwork more than a decade ago. Since then, we have gathered data from more than five thousand people. We have gathered the data by asking people in team-building seminars to provide us with two sets of information:

1. What is your best team experience? Describe the event you recall as being the most positive experience you have had working together with a group of people to achieve a common goal. It could be a family experience, a work group, a volunteer effort, a performing arts group, a military unit, an athletic team, a religious group, or any other setting that is characterized by team effort.

2. Identify the key elements of that most positive team experience. What characterized that team effort to make it so extraordinary?

Before reading any further, take a couple of minutes to think of your best "dream team" experience and answer, preferably in writing, the two questions above.

The thousands of responses we have received to these two simple questions form the core of this book. From the thousands of stories we have been told and the even greater number of characteristics of extraordinary team efforts that have been listed, we have identified seven common threads that seem to most often accompany great teamwork. These seven practices of great teams will provide the outline for expressing what we have learned from our experience and research on how to build and maintain extraordinary teamwork.

This "dream team experience" research brings to mind a couple of key points about teams. First, everyone is able to identify a "dream team" experience. We have all had them, even if they weren't televised! And since we have all had them, we understand that extraordinary teamwork is possible, even if we don't experience it very frequently. We already have an image of team excellence from our own experiences. Second, it is very interesting to observe people as they talk or write about their dream teams. If you were observing a room full of people exchanging stories about their dream teams, what would you expect to see? Time after time, we have observed enthusiasm, excitement, intensity, commitment, the will to win, and, overall, a lot of smiles. These were great experiences and people love to talk about them. In some cases, the experiences people report took place years, even decades ago. But when people recall their experience, they are excited and energized, even after long periods of time have passed.

Our goal is to get you to think about how you can create "dream team experiences" in your home, at your workplace, in community work, or in any other environment where you are working with others to achieve a common goal. It is possible for leaders—whether parents, managers, coaches, pastors, etc.—to lead in a manner that makes dream team experiences much more likely to occur. We will provide you with a structure for creating the magic of dream teams on a consistent, recurring basis. More specifically, the goals of this book are to:

- Contribute to your understanding of the dynamics of how extraordinary teams work

- Provide a broad structure for how to build seven team practices in a wide range of situations

- Provide a collaborative alternative to the traditional leadership model

- Provide the encouragement and motivation for you to embrace team concepts

In the next chapter, a brief introduction to each of the twelve dream team leaders we interviewed is provided. The following seven chapters are structured around each of the seven practices of dream teams. The final chapter summarizes the key ideas we believe to be most critical to creating and maintaining dream teams.

THE
REAL DREAM TEAM
LEADERS

As noted in the introduction, our search for core characteristics applicable to a broad range of team experiences began by gathering data on the dream team experiences of thousands of organizational leaders/managers. When this was completed, it resulted in an article in a management journal, presentations and proceedings articles at a couple of academic meetings, and a presentation and proceedings at a meeting of the International Academy of Management. Our work was favorably reviewed and received in these circles, which meant a lot to us. However, we were so excited about our newfound understanding of the power in the application of teaming concepts that we were not satisfied with the relatively small number of people with whom we had been able to share our results. Additionally, while the academic audiences found our work respectable, they accurately pointed out that we had not really discovered any major new theory of group dynamics.

As we analyzed our excitement, we became aware that the source of our enthusiasm for our work didn't come from any major theoretical breakthroughs. Instead,

17

it came from observing *the power available to every team leader—parents, teachers, managers, coaches, etc.—to become significantly more effective through the systematic application of what we already know about teams.* With this revelation, we realized we were sharing our ideas with the wrong people. Instead of focusing on communicating our ideas with academics, we needed to be talking with people who are more interested in *applications* than in theories.

Selection Of Twelve Real Dream Team Leaders

This application orientation led us to look for a group of twelve world-class leaders to interview whose stories might captivate the imagination of even the staunchest independent autocrat. These are our "real dream team leaders." It should be made clear that this selection process was based solely on the opinions of the authors. To make our list of twelve, a leader had to pass three tests.

First, we were looking for leaders whose team achievements distinguished them as being among the very best in the United States. We wanted people whose success as team leaders is not debatable—they have reached the top! That led us to a Nobel Prize winner, Medal of Honor recipient, best-in-industry winner, national championship coaches, etc. The second qualification was that the task of the team must clearly involve teamwork and close interdependence of the team members. The third qualification was that they be representative of a broad range of team efforts. This qualification led us to develop a list that included two business leaders, a football coach, an education leader, a minister, a biochemist, a pilot, a mountain climber, two basketball coaches, a musician, and a military leader. The diversity was desired to test the relevance of the seven practices of real dream teams that had been developed in the previous research. That is, are the same dynamics of team leadership at work in a mountain-climbing effort, a business, a symphonic orchestra, a basketball team, etc.?

Using this set of criteria, we developed our list of twelve "real dream team leaders" and set out to arrange personal, face-to-face interviews with each of them. Amazingly, of the original list of twelve, we were able to conduct in-depth interviews with nine (75 percent). Three other leaders were selected and interviewed to replace those who were unwilling to participate. We had wanted to talk with Ted Turner of Turner Broadcasting and the skipper of an America's Cup sailing team. When his office refused our request, we tried to visit with Dennis Conner, who also has America's Cup experience, but he was also unavailable. Another turn-down came from Robert Shaw, then conductor of the Atlanta Symphony Orchestra.

The only turn-down we still regret came from Sam Walton, the founder of Wal-Mart, who became the wealthiest man in America. We were very persistent in our attempts to gain his participation in this project. In fact, we actually spoke with him four different times (twice on the telephone and twice in person) in an attempt to gain his involvement. While we were able to convince him to take a full day to speak to a student group at our university, he persisted in his refusal to be featured in this book. In a personal conversation with Walton just a few months before his death, he told us his reason for denying our request:

> I would be more than glad to arrange for you to have as much time as you would need with David Glass [who is an outstanding Wal-Mart leader and the current CEO] or some other senior Wal-Mart leader. These leaders and the thousands of Wal-Mart associates are the reasons for the success of this company and for my success. I've already received way too much credit for this thing [the Wal-Mart phenomenon]. Please understand, I'm just not going to do anything that

would put me in the spotlight or cause me to receive any more credit.

What was most frustrating to us was that this attitude was exactly what we wanted to talk to him about, but we finally accepted his wishes and dropped our request. Sam Walton was a "real dream team leader," and his leadership style is the essence of what this book is about.

While there is plenty of room for discussion concerning who is the greatest business leader, woman basketball coach, business school dean, and so on, we hope you will agree that the twelve team leaders who were selected as the focus of this project are truly deserving of being designated "great." Allow us to introduce you to our twelve "Real Dream Team Leaders."

Lou Holtz

Lou Holtz coached the Fighting Irish, the Notre Dame University football team, to the NCAA Division I national championship in 1989 as well as several other outstanding top-ten seasons. His coaching career has also included amazing results at William and Mary, North Carolina State University, the University of Arkansas, and the University of Minnesota. In every case, Holtz inherited a program with a losing record and within two years had his team in a bowl game as recognition of their success.

Lou Holtz knows what it takes to build successful teams:

> To build a team you have to have a philosophy and you have to have a belief and you've got to believe it and you've got to operate by it. You can't change that philosophy one day or next week and say we're going to try this for awhile, you're going to run this slogan for a week and then you're going to have this theme for another week. You just can't have this! I think you decide what you want and you go and you preach it

and you preach it and you preach it and you believe it and you practice it and you practice it and you have confidence.

Holtz's philosophy is simple but powerful. The essence of his philosophy is captured in three rules or principles and three questions. The rules are as follows:

1. Do what's right. (Also known as the "do right" rule)

2. Always do your best.

3. Treat others as you would like to be treated. (The Golden Rule)

It is not that unusual for a team to say that these are their rules, but it is very unusual for a leader to demand that every member of the team always act on these rules. Holtz also has identified three questions that he believes everybody asks in a team environment, whether it be husbands and wives, parents and children, managers and workers, or coaches and players:

1. Can I trust you?

2. Are you committed to excellence?

3. Do you care about me?

We believe the Lou Holtz philosophy has much broader application than just winning football games, and apparently so do a lot of other people. During the off-season, corporate America and a host of other organizations have made Holtz one of the most widely sought motivational speakers. Talking with this football coach, teacher, humorist, and amateur magician reminded us again that real dream teams are not just sleight-of-hand magic. There is a structure and a method that will consistently build winning teams.

Major General Patrick Henry Brady

When we asked General Brady to define a hero, he gave the following response:

> A hero is somebody who...has a passionate love for other people or a cause...who really cares about other people and then puts that love and caring into action...above his or her own personal well-being. That's a hero!

Using that definition, our research led to the obvious conclusion that General Brady is a genuine, real-life, honest-to-goodness hero. As a "Dust-Off" helicopter pilot and commander of a medical evacuation unit during two tours of duty in Vietnam, Brady put his passionate love for other people into action time after time.

In one ten-month period his unit evacuated more injured patients (twenty thousand) than were carried during the entire Korean War. With six aircraft assigned to his unit at any one time, an average of seven were shot up every month. His forty-man detachment was awarded twenty-three Purple Hearts, and incredibly no one was killed.

In one day Brady flew three different helicopters (all three were hit by enemy fire) to evacuate a total of fifty-one seriously wounded men, many of whom would have perished without prompt medical treatment. For his courageous actions, he was awarded the nation's highest recognition for combat soldiers, the Medal of Honor.

Donald Petersen

Taking over as president and then CEO and chairman of the board in the early 1980s, Donald Petersen accepted the leadership role at Ford Motor Company at a time when things looked pretty bleak for the American automobile industry in general and Ford in particular. The American automobile industry was, to put it politely, getting kicked in the teeth by world competition, especially the Japanese. Not only were the costs of manufacturing making Ford products more expensive, but Ford's quality just wasn't good. Some irreverent Ford owners even joked that the letters FORD had taken on a new meaning: Fix Or Repair Daily. Another version was Found On Road Dead!

We interviewed Petersen in the spring of 1990, just a few weeks before his retirement. By that time, a whole new image of Ford Motor Company had emerged. The slogan "At Ford, Quality Is Job One" had achieved integrity of meaning. Now proud Ford owners were heard to say that FORD stands for First On Race Day! Petersen told us that Team Taurus, the project headed by Lew Veraldi, had been a major breakthrough for Ford Motor Company. As we listened to Petersen, and later Veraldi, we came to understand the significance of the paradigm shift that occurred with the change from "chimney thinking" to team thinking at Ford.

Petersen and Veraldi described the traditional organization and project processes as a linear structure that was analogous to a series of side-by-side chimneys trying to work together. There was the design engineering chimney, the process engineering chimney, the marketing chimney, the finance chimney, etc. Using this method to design a new automobile required passing ideas from the bottom of one chimney to top of that chimney, then across to the top of the next chimney, and then down to the bottom and back to the top, etc. Suffice it to say that if you're having a hard time following this process, so did the people at Ford! The contribution of Team Taurus was to break down the chimneys and move away from a sequential, linear process to an interactive, concentric process. Team Taurus was made up of cross-functional members from design engineering, product engineering, process engineering, marketing, finance, service, and other areas that have to work together to produce an automobile. All of these people were involved in creating the Taurus from the beginning of the process to the end of the process.

Did the concept work? In 1993, Taurus replaced the Honda Accord as the best-selling automobile in the United States. The Taurus project initiated under the leadership of Petersen (as well as other less famous experiments based on the same concept) has revolutionized American industry.

As reported in the introduction, Petersen told us that his legacy to Ford Motor Company was that "people at Ford work together differently than they did a few years ago when I assumed leadership—they work as teams." We asked him if that meant 90 to 100 percent of people were sold on the team philosophy. His answer was:

> Oh no, probably more like 40 percent, but that is enough. Those people comprise a critical mass of evangelists who know the truth about how to work together, and they will convert the others. I feel pleased that 40 percent believe in teams.

That's pretty visionary as well as tough-minded leadership.

We believe Donald Petersen is a great role model for excellence in corporate leadership. John W. Gardner, who has spent decades leading and studying leaders, agrees. His book *Leaders* is one of the most insightful books on leadership. We attended a national conference where Gardner gave the keynote address and discussed the leadership qualities of great leaders in American history. At the conclusion of his presentation he took questions from the audience. One of us (Bob) asked him the following question: "You talked about great leaders like Thomas Jefferson, Abraham Lincoln, and others from our past. Why don't we have any leaders like that today? Why can't leaders be great today?" Gardner replied:

We do have great leaders today, they're just harder to recognize. I'll just give you one example of a great leader that I have observed—Donald Petersen at Ford, now he is a truly exceptional leader!

At that point, we put Petersen on our list of people to interview, and we weren't disappointed. The examples and stories that follow provide just a brief glance into the team leadership orientation that has led Ford Motor Company to the front of the pack in the automobile industry.

Lou Whittaker

When we first conceived the idea of studying teamwork by looking at great leaders, we quickly decided that mountaineering was one area of teamwork on which we wanted to focus. Our first thought was that we should interview Jim Whittaker (Lou's twin brother), who in 1963 became the first American to reach the summit of the world's tallest mountain, Mt. Everest (29,000+ feet).

In discussing this idea with Bob East, a knowledgeable mountaineering friend of ours, he agreed that Jim Whittaker was probably the most famous climber in the United States. However, he then proceeded to talk about Lou Whittaker and suggested he would also be an excellent interview. We told him we were looking for great leaders whose teams had achieved truly spectacular results. We asked if Lou Whittaker had ever stood at the summit of Mt. Everest, like his brother Jim had done. Bob East's reply crystallized a classic principle of team leadership. He said, "No, he has never stood at the summit of Everest himself, but as a leader he has put other people on top."

We found Lou Whittaker in Ashford, Washington, at the foot of Mt. Rainier. Lou makes his home near there and is known locally as "Mr. Mt. Rainier" because of his knowledge of and experience on the mountain. Whittaker has led climbs all over the world, including Mt. Everest, K-2, Mt. McKinley, and numerous others. In 1984, Whittaker led the first all-American team to the summit of Mt. Everest, which at over 29,000 feet is considered to be the highest elevation in the world.

When we asked Whittaker to describe his best team experience, he quickly pointed to the 1984 Mt. Everest climb, even though he personally never stood at the summit. Interestingly, Lou has stood at the summit of Mt. McKinley, whose vertical rise from base to summit is greater than that of Mt. Everest, but he didn't mention that until questioned directly. Referring to the 1984 Everest experience, Whittaker said, "I led the climb that made the successful ascent. That gave me the satisfaction of placing the first team on top. It was as fulfilling as doing it myself." When we pushed a little harder on the question of who goes to the summit and who supports, Whittaker told us, "If any member of the team makes it to the top, then every team member has made it to the top."

Gertrude Elion

In 1988, Gertrude Elion, along with Dr. George Hitchings and Sir James Black, received the Nobel Prize in Physiology or Medicine. The award to Elion was in recognition of her life's work, which included seeking a cure for leukemia. As a biochemist at Burroughs Wellcome Company in Raleigh, North Carolina, Dr. Elion labored tirelessly in her attempts to discover a treatment or a cure to prevent the special pain and cruelty that are associated with diseases such as this one, which predominately strikes children. During her career, Dr. Elion's teams made major contributions to the field of medicine by developing a drug that made kidney transplants possible, in addition to drugs to treat gout, herpes, chicken pox, and shingles.

Elion's selection for the Nobel Medal was a long shot for several reasons. First, she is obviously a woman in a field (biochemistry) that has been dominated by males. Second, Gertrude Elion never completed her doctorate degree. In the early 1950s, the dean of the Ph.D. program in which she was enrolled insisted that she leave her job at Burroughs Wellcome and come back to school full time to complete her work on her doctorate. Elion told us that even then she felt she was making great progress in her leukemia research, so she refused to leave her work and dropped out of the Ph.D. program. Not having a doctorate degree represents a major sacrifice for any research scientist. One might become embittered toward the university that forced this type of choice, but what tells you a lot about Gertrude Elion is that after she received the Nobel Prize she graciously accepted an honorary doctorate from that same school and even made a personal contribution to the academic scholarship fund. The third strike should have been that she conducted her research in a private, for-profit, proprietary organization. It is extremely rare for anyone not associated with a research university to win a Nobel Prize in Physiology or Medicine.

But this woman in a "man's world," without a Ph.D. in a field where a degree is assumed, working for a corporation rather than a university, overcame all of the odds. And the way she did it shows a deep understanding of teamwork and an uncompromising, total commitment to a very worthy mission.

Jody Conradt

There are several great women's basketball programs around—the University of Tennessee, Louisiana Tech, and Henderson State to name just a few. Year in and year out, Jody Conradt's Lady Longhorns from the University of Texas will be as competitive as any. Why? As with the other dream teams, it has to do with having a leader who knows how to build a team. The Lady Longhorns went undefeated for over a decade in the Southwest Conference, and the Lady Longhorns of 1985-86 may have been the best women's basketball team of all time. With a record of thirty-six wins and no losses, this real dream team stormed to the NCAA Division I national championship.

Coach Conradt sees her job as being much bigger than winning basketball games. She describes her job more in terms of developing young women than in terms of sports:

> I think what I would really like for them to feel is a sense of team, and that it's positive to be involved with a group of people who can set aside personal feelings for the good of the group. And I think that those are the feelings that they probably take with them longer than anything else. "I was a part of something that was memorable, something that was special because it was hard, but it was also fun."...and it's critical for every individual on every team to realize that you can do more than you think you can do!

When asked what it takes to build a championship effort, Conradt had a ready response:

> It takes people who are willing to sacrifice self for the good of the group and that means passing sometimes when you want to shoot. That means playing defense, sacrificing the ability to go as hard as you could offensively because you've extended yourself defensively. I think that's a very basic thing. And there's a real need to reinforce...that selfishness and ego will kill a team. What we really need is a team ego and we have to portray that and we have to protect that.
>
> On a team, you start out trying to please the coaches, your teammates, and the fans, but all that changes. By the time you've gone through the whole [team] process, at the end you realize that what you're really trying to do is please yourself...but your approach and your intensity and your focus has changed

and you figure out what [the team] is trying to accomplish and what you have to do to get [the team] there.

Former Texas Congresswoman Barbara Jordan summed up the 1985-86 Lady Longhorns' accomplishments in her congratulatory speech at the national championship celebration: "You have shown all of America something very special. You have shown them a TEAM!"

Don Tyson

The Tyson Foods story is one of tremendous growth, high-quality products, and astounding profitability. From 1983 to 1993, the number of people working at Tyson Foods grew from less than 10,000 to more than 56,000 and revenues increased from 603 million to almost 5 billion dollars. The company has consistently won industry awards for the quality of its products. During a recent ten-year period, Tyson Foods was the most profitable company in the Fortune 500, with an average return to shareholders of 52 percent per year.

At the heart of the Tyson story is the senior chairman of the board and visionary leader of the company, Don Tyson. When we asked Don Tyson to describe the key to his success in leading Tyson Foods, his response focused on people and teamwork. "There's no way we could have done all this without everyone working hard, doing his or her best." His respect for *all* Tyson people is bone-deep—and genuine. If you were to walk into Don Tyson's Springdale, Arkansas, office, which is a replica of the White House Oval Office during Jimmy Carter's presidency, you would see the senior chairman of the board wearing a khaki uniform with the name "Don" embroidered on his shirt.

Everyone at Tyson Foods wears a khaki uniform with his or her first name on one side and the Tyson logo on the other. In the early years, before the company became so large and well-known, the senior managers would wear

business suits whenever Wall Street analysts or New York
bankers came to town. Today, it is a rare occasion to find
anyone out of uniform. The uniforms have come to sym-
bolize the egalitarian values of teamwork that are at the
heart of Don Tyson's philosophy of living and the success
of Tyson Foods.

Steve Trent

At the time of our interview, Lt. Col. Steve Trent was
serving as the commander/lead pilot for the Thunderbird
Flight Demonstration Team of the U.S. Air Force. The
Thunderbirds perform intricate maneuvers as they fly
F-16 jets at 500 m.p.h, sometimes with wings overlapped, as close as eighteen inches apart. In this environment, teamwork becomes an immediate life or death
issue.

At the time of our interview, Trent had logged over
three thousand hours in fighter aircraft, including over
five hundred hours in combat, and had participated in a
three-year exchange program with the U.S. Navy. During
his Navy tour, Trent was selected to attend the elite flight
training program at Miramar, California, which the Navy
calls the "Fighter Weapons School" and the flyers call
"Top Gun." The movie *Top Gun* was based on that school
and the competition among the pilots for the first-in-class
award which goes to the most elite of the elite—the "Top
Gun." Steve Trent is a real, live "Top Gun." He was first
in his piloting training class and first in his fighter training class. But Steve Trent couldn't be more unlike the
character Maverick (played by Tom Cruise) in the movie.
If you've seen the movie, you may recall that Maverick
was a fiercely independent, self-oriented character who
caused his partner's death because he was hot-dogging
when he should have been supporting another flight team.
Steve Trent exudes the characteristics of real dream team
leaders—a clear sense of mission, support, trust, coop-

eration, competency, a winning attitude, and more. His response to our stock first question—"What does it take to build a successful team?"—set the team-oriented tone of the interview:

> Well, it's a pretty complex subject....I think it depends on the situation as well as the people involved and their dedication to making a good team. By situational I mean if you're put in a position where you must work together as a team, whether it be some sort of survival type scenario, a prisoner of war scenario, or in our case, where you are traveling together for 250 days a year and you need everybody's best effort to make the mission successful....If we need to call on external help rather than blunder through, we will. But the fact that we're pretty self-reliant and that we have a mission that is important tends to draw us together and you can rely on each other more and you start building a team spirit. Then you could stop right there if you don't have the right attitudes [the attitude that everyone on the team is important]—like the guy at work who feels that he doesn't have a contribution and that nobody else is relying on him, so he doesn't work hard or enjoy his work. Yet the same guy goes to the softball team at the church where they are relying on him to make the base hit and drive in the winning run and he gets really excited about the softball team.

Application of the dream team practices, in settings ranging from air shows to working at an office or plant to the church softball team, becomes apparent as the real dream team leaders tell their stories.

Sybil Mobley

Dr. Sybil Mobley is one busy woman. It took us two years to arrange a visit with her—and then it was with the knowledge that a Hershey Foods' corporate jet was waiting to whisk her away to a meeting of the Hershey board of directors the next day. Hershey Foods is not the only company that values Dr. Mobley's advice. She has served on the board of directors of Sears, Southwestern Bell, and Premark International, among other companies.

Dr. Mobley's career has not always been so glamorous. In fact, at one time she was a clerk typist in the business office of Florida A&M University; now she serves as dean. Sybil Mobley modeled the way for her students of today with a "can do" commitment to personal development and excellence by returning to graduate school and earning her MBA from the Wharton School and her Ph.D. from the University of Illinois before joining the Florida A&M faculty and eventually becoming dean.

Under her leadership, Florida A&M's business school has become one of the top ten business schools in the United States. The entire student experience is organized around working together in teams. Students are required to do *two* summer internships, one domestic and one international. Recent graduates of the school received an average of seven job offers each from Fortune 500 companies.

Norman Vincent Peale

Dr. Norman Vincent Peale has several claims to fame. Most people know him as the author of *The Power of Positive Thinking,* one of the best-selling non-fiction books of all time, with sales approaching fifteen million copies. He also served as pastor of Marble Collegiate Church, the oldest Protestant church in New York City, for an incredible fifty-two years! One church with the same pastor for fifty-two years must be some kind of record. When Dr. Peale finally decided to leave Marble Collegiate Church at an age when most people would have been retired for many years, he and his wife, Ruth Stafford Peale, continued their work with two organizations which they founded, the Peale Center for Christian Living and *Guidepost* magazine, which has a monthly circulation of over four million copies.

As impressed as we were with all of these accomplishments, we were most impressed with his sixty-three-year marriage partnership that endured until his death in December 1993 at the age of ninety-five. When we called to arrange an interview, we explained that we were interested in team issues and the role they have played in his life. Dr. Peale suggested that Mrs. Peale also be present for the interview. We told him we didn't really think that would be necessary. He quickly told us we were mistaken, and we just as quickly agreed that her presence would be most welcomed.

As the interview progressed, it became very apparent why Dr. Peale had insisted that Mrs. Peale be present. These two were a great team! They described how they had worked together to raise a beautiful family and how they had supported each other in their work. Dr. Peale told us that *The Power of Positive Thinking* would probably never have been written if not for Ruth's editing and transcribing work. Much of the book is based on sermons he had preached, and on some occasions, he was so self-critical that he would put his notes away and never look at them again. Ruth told us how she had taken the tapes of the sermons and organized, transcribed, edited, and prepared them for proofing.

Dr. Peale's contribution to helping people understand the power of the human mind is a great gift to humanity. His belief that positive thinking results in higher levels of achievement is an extension of the statement by William James: "The greatest discovery of this generation is that a human being can change his life by changing his attitude of mind." The next extension of this thinking is that a team can change its outcomes by changing its attitude of mind, its mental model for teamwork.

Our interview with Dr. Peale brought a spiritual dimension to the concept of great teamwork. His message seemed to be that faith in self, faith in others, and faith in God generate the spirit of hope and expectancy that we call a winning attitude.

Carl Schiebler

The New York Philharmonic Orchestra is comprised of the world's greatest musicians. That may sound a bit subjective, but that's our opinion after attending a rehearsal, conducting a couple of interviews, and attending a performance at Avery Fisher Hall in New York. There are certainly many other great symphony orchestras—Berlin, Chicago, London, and Atlanta, just to name a few. But when a vacancy occurs in the New York Philharmonic, it is not unusual to receive applications from the top musicians in these other outstanding orchestras, which suggests, as Schiebler put it, that "this is the top of the heap."

As director of personnel for the orchestra, Carl Schiebler is responsible for coordinating many of the human resource functions and services, including recruitment and selection of orchestra members. Carl graciously agreed to talk with us after our scheduled interview with conductor Zubin Mehta had to be canceled due to a brief illness. Before coming to his current role with the New York Philharmonic, Schiebler played the French horn as a member of the St. Louis Symphony.

His experience as an individual professional musician and as a person with leadership/administrative responsibilities for the entire orchestra gives him special insight into the extraordinary challenge of taking 106 talented individual artists and blending their efforts into harmonious music. On one hand, the orchestra requires the very best in individual effort and talent. At the same time, these artists must be willing to cooperate in a manner that subverts their individuality to the common good. Schiebler puts it this way:

...you're supposed to be interpretative and be an individual interpreting the art. Then you carry this a few steps further and you get into a symphony orchestra...and you get in on one of the last dictatorships on earth. And so you have these 106 totally individually trained, free-thinking [people who] play it for themselves—"I play it like I play it."...Music is very, very defined and it's very disciplined because of rhythms and time and notes and stuff like that. But within that there is a framework of a little bit of elasticity, and you train them to do that. Well, then you put them in a symphony orchestra and you take one person that stands up on a podium and says, "Gosh, I'm glad you're all great artists. I'm glad you're all such great individuals. Now, we're going to do it my way!"

Asked to describe what it feels like to be a part of a symphony orchestra, Schiebler painted a clear picture:

It's a family, oh yeah! A symphony orchestra is like...a small town, a small isolated town. You have older people, you have younger people, you have the far right, you have the far left, you've got radicals, you've got conservatives, all different age groups. One thing brings them together. Absolutely. And you have to remember that's what you're focused on—it's the art, it's their performance. We're [the support staff] here for them and they're here for the art. They're not here just for themselves, uh-uh, it's bigger than that!

John Wooden

John Wooden's record as a basketball coach is unequaled. Consider the accomplishments of his UCLA basketball Bruins:

- Ten NCAA championships—1964, 1965, 1967, 1968, 1969, 1970, 1971, 1972, 1973, 1975

- Seven consecutive NCAA championships (next best is two)

- Thirty-eight consecutive NCAA Tournament victories (next best is thirteen)

- Eighty-eight consecutive victories (next best is sixty)

- Eight undefeated Pac-8 Conference championships (no other team has ever gone undefeated in conference play)

Some have explained his success by pointing out that he had great players such as Bill Walton and Kareem Abdul-Jabbar. But other teams have had great players. Ohio State won an NCAA championship in 1960 with three future NBA greats. John Havlicek (sophomore), Jerry Lucas (sophomore), and Larry Siegfried (junior) combined with Mel Nowell and Joe Roberts to create a force that experts said would lead to three straight championships, but even with these tremendous talents, the Buckeyes were unable to win another championship. More recently, the "Fab 5" from the University of Michigan were touted as having the potential to win two or three championships, but a lack of teamwork and a lack of commitment on the part of these extraordinarily talented young men to stay with the team for four years resulted in no championship.

They say Wooden built a dynasty that allowed him to recruit "all the good players," forgetting that he was only allowed to have twelve to fifteen players on his team each year. Still others say that there is greater parity in the game today and that it is not possible for any team to match the accomplishments of Coach Wooden's teams. Wooden's response to this type of speculation is almost uncharacteristically straightforward and bold: "I think it's just as possible for it to happen now as it was then!"

John Wooden's "Pyramid of Success" is a great tool

for conceptualizing teamwork. In fact, his book, *They Call Me Coach*, contains some of the best insight around for managers and leaders. In the book, Coach Wooden defines team spirit as "a genuine consideration for others— an eagerness to sacrifice personal interests or glory for the welfare of all." At the top of the pyramid is "competitive greatness—be your best when your best is needed— enjoyment of a difficult challenge." When all the building blocks are present, a team has the potential to achieve "success—peace of mind which is a direct result of self-satisfaction in knowing you did your best to become the best that you are capable of becoming..."

The Seven Practices Of Real Dream Teams

The thousands of descriptions of dream teams combined with the interviews we conducted with the real dream team leaders revealed countless good ideas about how to create and maintain real dream teams. In an effort to organize our thinking, we have identified the common themes that exist throughout the ideas. These themes, or common threads, have resulted in the identification of seven categories of common practices of real dream teams. These practices can also be referred to as "the threads of teamwork" because they must *all* be woven together to create the real dream team fabric. If one thread is missing, the whole fabric is in danger of coming unraveled. Each of the threads or practices will be the subject of one of the next seven chapters, but first we provide a quick overview of the seven threads that comprise the real dream team fabric.

Commitment To A Clear Mission

At the core of the success of real dream teams is a clear understanding in the minds of all team members of why

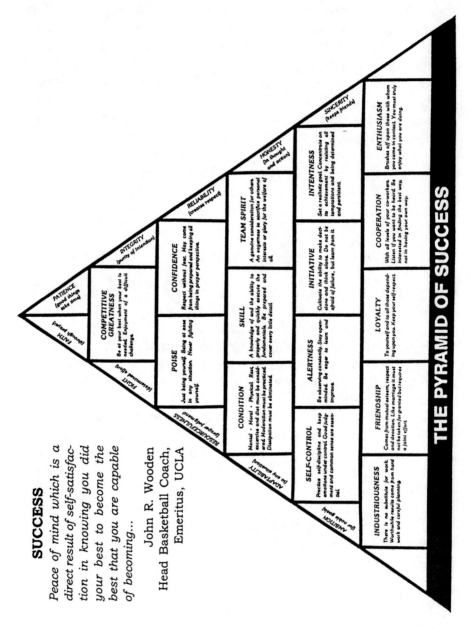

SUCCESS

Peace of mind which is a direct result of self-satisfaction in knowing you did your best to become the best that you are capable of becoming...

John R. Wooden
Head Basketball Coach,
Emeritus, UCLA

THE PYRAMID OF SUCCESS

FAITH (through prayer)

PATIENCE (good things take time)

COMPETITIVE GREATNESS — Be at your best when your best is needed. Enjoyment of a difficult challenge.

INTEGRITY (purity of intention)

RELIABILITY (creates respect)

CONFIDENCE — Respect without fear. May come from being prepared and keeping all things in proper perspective.

POISE — Just being yourself. Being at ease in any situation. Never fighting yourself.

FIGHT (determined effort)

HONESTY (in thought and action)

TEAM SPIRIT — A genuine consideration for others. An eagerness to sacrifice personal interests or glory for the welfare of all.

SKILL — A knowledge of and the ability to properly and quickly execute the fundamentals. Be prepared and cover every little detail.

RESOURCEFULNESS (proper judgment)

SINCERITY (keeps friends)

INTENTNESS — Set a realistic goal. Concentrate on its achievement by resisting all temptations and being determined and persistent.

INITIATIVE — Cultivate the ability to make decisions and think alone. Do not be afraid of failure, but learn from it.

ALERTNESS — Be observing constantly. Stay open-minded. Be eager to learn and improve.

CONDITION — Mental - Moral - Physical. Rest, exercise and diet must be considered. Moderation must be practiced. Dissipation must be eliminated.

ADAPTABILITY (to any situation)

ENTHUSIASM — Brushes off upon those with whom you come in contact. You must truly enjoy what you are doing.

COOPERATION — With all levels of your co-workers. Listen if you want to be heard. Be interested in finding the best way, not in having your own way.

LOYALTY — To yourself and to all those depending upon you. Keep your self-respect.

FRIENDSHIP — Comes from mutual esteem, respect and devotion. Like marriage it must not be taken for granted but requires a joint effort.

INDUSTRIOUSNESS — There is no substitute for work. Worthwhile results come from hard work and careful planning.

SELF-CONTROL — Practice self-discipline and keep emotions under control. Good judgment and common sense are essential.

AMBITION (for noble goals)

THE PYRAMID OF SUCCESS

the team exists. This understanding is accompanied by a deep commitment to the mission, which is derived from the general belief that "what we're doing is important—it's worth my life."

Mutual Support And Encouragement

"You can count on me, especially when you need me" captures the essence of the interrelationship of dream team members. Real dream team members encourage and support each other at levels that create the freedom which allows people to give their best effort with no fear that their own teammates will become the enemy.

Clearly Defined Roles

A wide range of diverse skills, knowledge, values, and attitudes are required for team success. A respect for and acceptance of the need for diversity, accompanied by the ability to clearly define "who does what," creates the magic or synergy of everyone working together. When roles are clearly defined and aligned, the idea that "none of us is as good as all of us" becomes operational.

Win-Win Cooperation

Cooperation can best be defined as an attitude that asks questions such as, "What can I do for you? What are your needs? What is in the best interest of the whole team? How can I help?" This "all for one, one for all" type of thinking is the glue that holds real dream teams together.

Individual Competency

The individuals who comprise real dream teams are committed to personal excellence—becoming the best they can be in their roles. They work hard, focus on the fundamentals, and are relentless in their pursuit of personal improvement and growth.

Empowering Communication

In more than 90 percent of the teams we have worked with in team-building sessions, the number one issue and barrier to success is lack of effective communication. Real dream teams are different; they have discovered one of the key secrets of effective teamwork: people on real dream teams just talk to each other. And they talk to each other about any issue, positive or negative, which affects team performance. The norm is that any news is good news as long as it helps us to be more successful.

Winning Attitude

No team wins every time, but real dream teams *expect* to win every time. Their winning expectations create confidence, focus, and high levels of motivation. As a result, they end up winning more often than a logical assessment of their talent would suggest.

The Seven Practices Template

The Seven Practices Template can be used as the "mental model" for gauging your team's effectiveness. High and sustained use of each practice is your evidence of real dream team effort.

LOW ⟶ *Commitment To A Clear Mission* ⟶ *HIGH*	
Low visibility	Highly visible
Low value for organization	Shared energizer for organization
No conscious alignment of systems and actions with mission	The force around which systems and actions align

LOW ⟶ *Mutual Support And Encouragement* ⟶ *HIGH*	
Low team confidence	Faith that others are working with you toward common goals
Visible acts of distrust	Visible acts of trust
Energy directed toward turf protection	Energy directed toward winning

LOW ⟶ *Clearly Defined Roles* ⟶ *HIGH*	
Vague and unconnected to mission	Clear and connected to mission
Expectations unclarified	Expectations clarified for all, shared by all
Confusion as to responsibilities	

LOW ⟶ *Win–Win Cooperation* ⟶ *HIGH*	
Win–lose scenarios	High evidence of working toward common mission
Get others before they get you	Open dialogue around win–win opportunities
Unintended negative consequences	Intentional "systems thinking"

LOW ⟶ *Individual Competency* ⟶ HIGH	
Low organizational value placed on technical, inter-personal, team competencies	High organizational value placed on technical, inter-personal, team competencies

LOW ⟶ *Empowering Communication* ⟶ HIGH	
Key information withheld	All business information shared freely
Communication sluggish and defensive	Communication responses speedy and non-defensive

LOW ⟶ *Winning Attitude* ⟶ HIGH	
Team feels discouraged	Team expects to win or reach mission
Low energy	Enthusiasm openly shared
Victimized and dependent on external resources	Confident of internal strengths

"IS WHAT YOU'RE DOING IMPORTANT?"

PRACTICE #1:
COMMITMENT TO
A CLEAR MISSION

Extraordinary results begin with somebody's dream. Before a true mission can exist, someone must have a dream, and the dream must be shared and embraced by the team members. We all have dreams for our families, for ourselves, and for the organizations we lead. However, what seems to separate the twelve real dream team leaders from most people is their level of aspiration, the scope of their dreams, and the tenacity with which they hold on to their dreams—they just don't give up!

Henry Ford dreamed of an automobile for every American. Donald Petersen dreamed of a quality automobile for every American. We were eager to learn what Ford Motor Company had done under Petersen's leadership in the early 1980s to make "Quality Job One" at Ford, especially after the negative reputation that had developed in the 1960s and 1970s. "What did you do to turn Ford around?" we asked Petersen. Before the question was

43

completed, he was reaching for his inside coat pocket from which he produced a laminated card containing a statement of Ford's mission and values—the seeds of the Ford revolution. His dream had been captured in these statements and set in motion on a long weekend retreat several years before. He told us it had taken more than five years to develop a "critical mass" of believers who shared his dream at Ford.

The leaders of great teams seem to have the ability to create a sense of mission for the teams they lead. This leadership ability is sometimes treated as an almost mystical quality that is only available to heroes and superhumans—but that simply is not the case. This ability can be captured by "regular" parents, managers, spouses, community leaders, and in other team situations; it yields a powerful tool for achieving extraordinary results.

The leaders of real dream teams seem to have at least four characteristics that enable them to bring out the best efforts in people. First, they seem to have a sense of *vision* which allows them to view things differently than most people. This visionary ability is characterized by a "mountain-top" view, a futuristic/long-term view, and a strong belief in the importance of "the cause." Their mountain-top view allows them to see the forest rather than just the trees; they see the complexity of issues and seek out and solve the intricate relationships among systems. H.L. Mencken once said that "for every problem there is a solution that is simple, direct, and wrong!" These effective leaders avoid overly simplistic solutions that don't work. They seek out difficult challenges and then stick with it until the job is done. John F. Kennedy's classic visionary challenge contained in his inaugural address is an example of the desire and ability to look at problems from a different perspective: "Some people see things as they are and ask why? Others see things as they should be and ask why not?"

While visionary thinking is the beginning of team greatness, it is not enough by itself. Leaders must have the ability to communicate the vision to others. Martin Luther King had a vision of how things could and should be; his "I Have a Dream" speech is widely regarded as one of the most powerful, influential communication events. In that speech, he described his dream:

> I say to you today, my friends, so even though we face the difficulties of today and tomorrow, I still have a dream. It is deeply rooted in the American dream.
>
> I have a dream that one day this nation will rise up and live out the true meaning of its creed: "We hold these truths to be self-evident; that all men are created equal." I have a dream that one day on the red hills of Georgia that the sons of former slaves and the sons of former slaveowners will be able to sit down together at the table of brotherhood.
>
> I have a dream that my four little children will one day live in a nation where they will not be judged by the color of their skin but by the content of their character....This is our hope....
>
> And when this happens, and when we allow freedom to ring, when we let it ring from every village and every hamlet, from every state and every city, we will be able to speed up that day when all of God's children, black men and white men, Jews and Gentiles, Protestants and Catholics, will be able to join hands and sing in the words of the old Negro spiritual, "Free at last! Free at last! Thank God Almighty, we're free at last!"

King drew the picture; he communicated the vision. As a consequence, millions of people who had little hope of things ever getting any better gained hope. When the leader has a great vision and communicates it, thereby generating *hope*, a mission is created. For a mission to truly drive a cause or an organization, there must be hope.

The third characteristic these leaders possess is the ability to empower and involve others in achieving the mission. They recognize that they cannot achieve the mission alone. They fully utilize the resources of the team. They listen to and build up others. They share power, and in the process they actually become more powerful. They take their dreams and organize them into reality, so they are able to come true. Sam Walton's dream of building the most successful retail company in the world only became reality as a result of organizing and implementing his dream. He built a team of outstanding people who were empowered by sharing his vision. Through their commitment and effort, Wal-Mart grew from one small store in rural Arkansas to the world's largest retailer in less than thirty years.

The fourth mission-related characteristic that these people personify is especially difficult to label. Is it dedication, discipline, faith, self-motivation, or commitment? It is probably all of the above. As we interviewed these leaders and listened to them describe their greatest team experiences, it became clear that these men and women are *different*! They know why they exist, they know what they're doing, and, most of all, they communicate an unwavering, uncompromising commitment to achieving a mission which is capable of inspiring others to do their best. John Wooden, Don Tyson, Sybil Mobley, Jody Conradt, Lou Whittaker, and all the others exude a dedication and commitment that cause the uncommitted to feel uncomfortable, perhaps even a bit embarrassed, in their presence.

Nowhere did we see a greater dedication and commitment to the mission than in the life of Gertrude Elion. We asked Dr. Elion, now in her seventies, to think back over her life and tell us if she had any regrets about the way she had lived her life to this point. This great woman, who has been single for her entire life, thought for a second and then simply said, "children." We followed up, asking her to clarify this comment. As her eyes glistened, she went on to explain:

> I love children. I would have loved to have had children of my own—a daughter or son. But I just couldn't do it—my work was so important—I decided that I couldn't do both. I decided that the best way for me to show my love for children was through finding a treatment or cure for this terrible disease. So I never took the time to be married and to have children. But I would have loved to have had children.

Can you imagine that level of commitment? Most of us probably cannot. While we are not advocating that everyone give up their families so they can focus on nothing but their work, we present this story as an example of the level of commitment we encountered in visiting with these real dream team leaders.

Creating A Clear Sense Of Mission

Whether you review the ideas of the great ancient philosophers such as Plato, Aristotle, and Socrates or ask a modern-day philosopher at a liberal arts university, you are likely to get the same response if you ask them to identify the most important question a man or woman confronts in life. They will probably tell you that *the* big question in life is "Why do I exist?" Individuals who have confronted, wrestled with, and answered this question to their own satisfaction typically exhibit high levels of motivation, self-confidence, and a strong sense of direction. They know where they are going! Stephen Covey, in his widely read *The Seven Habits of Highly Effective People*, clearly underscores the effectiveness of having a personal mission or "beginning with the end in mind." The message is to focus your energy on the important stuff!

The great management philosophers tell us that this same question—why do we exist?—is the most important question teams answer—or don't answer. Peter Drucker, perhaps the most widely respected management philosopher of this century, has observed that while nothing may seem simpler or more obvious than the "why" question, "managerial neglect of this question is the most important single cause of organization frustration and failure." In his experience, "when the concept of an organization's business [or reason for being] is not thought through and spelled out clearly, the enterprise lacks a solid foundation for establishing realistic objectives, strategies, plans, and work assignments" (Drucker, 1973, p. 77).

A shared common goal as a powerful builder of group cohesion has always emerged from group dynamics research. The figure below depicts the lack of a common sense of direction that exists in many groups. The large arrow represents the general direction desired by the team's leadership. The small arrows represent the efforts of the individuals who constitute the team. While some of the team members are going in the desired direction, some are directing their work at an angle to the optimum and some are even pulling against the team's mission.

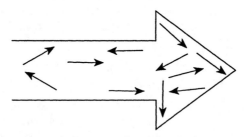

People sometimes deliberately pull against the team or organization because the organizational goals may not be compatible with their individual goals. In a few cases, people may become so embittered toward the leader or others that they want the organization to fail. More often, however, the problem is not one of people deliberately working against one another and the organization. Instead, the lack of concerted effort is a natural by-product of team members simply *not knowing* the overall direction of the team and how they can contribute to its success. A basic assumption of the application of team concepts is the assumption of good intentions. That is, most people in the organization go to work every day with high internal motivation, wanting to win, and looking for the opportunity to make a positive contribution to the success of the team. It then becomes a key leadership/management responsibility to identify a clear sense of direction and to facilitate the alignment of personal goals with the organization's general mission. The figure below suggests the synergistic increase in power that occurs when this process is managed properly.

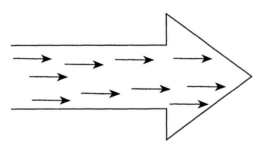

This sense of oneness, or pulling together and knowing where you are going, is the opposite of the frustration that is expressed in the 1970s film *Bonnie and Clyde.* Toward the end of their exploits and shortly before their violent deaths, a disenchanted Bonnie tells her partner Clyde, "I always thought we was going somewhere, but I guess we was just going."

While the other characteristics of great teams have the potential to contribute significantly to achieving this oneness phenomenon, none has greater potential than the establishment of a clear sense of direction through a common mission. This, of course, is not a new idea. Henri

Fayol, one of the founders of contemporary management thought, wrote about it in 1916. In *Administration industriell et generale* (*General and Industrial Management*), he described what he called the "unity of management" principles. According to Fayol, there should be one manager and one plan for all operations which have the same object in view. The manager's job is to see that all efforts are directed toward the same end.

Fayol's idea is simple but powerful, especially if one goes beyond such typical management phrases as common direction or common goal and focuses instead on the more dynamic, competitive term mission. The managers and real dream team leaders we interviewed weren't just working toward a shared sense of direction. They were on a mission!

Sybil Mobley isn't just trying to make the Florida A&M School of Business better. She has a clearly defined mission to change for the better the lives of the young men and women whom she views as her responsibility. One need only ask the people who were around her as she built the school's great program and faculty—she was on a crusade to achieve a mission.

Lou Whittaker was doing more than leading a team in the common direction of the top of Mt. Everest. As they endured incredible hardship, camping for months in small tents, facing unbearable weather, and existing in a rarefied atmosphere that creates almost constant pain, these men and women actually put their lives at risk as a matter of routine. They knew too well from their past experience that the consequence of one small mistake could be instant death for themselves or their teammates. But they endured the hardship, they accepted the pain, and they took the risks. Why? Because they were on a mission that would take them to the top of the world.

When we talked with General Brady about his experience in rescuing the wounded in Vietnam, he said that a sense of mission was critical in enabling him and his people to take the risks they needed to take.

> ...dedication to our fighting troops, to save their lives. That was the mission...we were very close knit because every tough mission was a great victory for us. It was like winning the championship because you went out, things were very, very tense, people were nervous, always a lot of confusion, people hurt, and how in the heck are we going to do this, and how are we going to get through these obstacles. And then all of a sudden it's over and you've got to get him back, and then he's in the hospital, and they're all in the hospital. Then you just take a big sigh of relief!

Brady went on to talk about how a strong sense of mission works to pull diverse people together:

> You'll find people...who can be as strange bedfellows as you'll ever want to meet. They can be weird in many ways but when it comes to the mission...they are all focused. They don't take themselves seriously and they don't take most other things seriously, unless it's time for that mission. They are fanatics when it comes to mission.

Nothing has more potential to pull a team together than the development of, and the focus on, a common mission. People can be fanatics about the mission. In working with a variety of groups, we have observed teams that exhibit varying levels of cohesion. Some are able to endure tremendous hardship without complaining. Others seem to whine and bicker at the first hint of any difficulty.

A classic "Pogo" cartoon from the 1970s makes the point well. As with many of his statements, Pogo seemed more intent on challenging us than providing amusement. The cartoon was a simple two frames. The setting in frame one showed Pogo standing in a mud hole, looking down at the huge mess surrounding him. The second frame showed Pogo in the same situation but looking up at a beautiful blue sky filled with birds, a few fleecy white clouds, and a bright sun. The captions were simple:

Frame 1: "You can spend your whole life looking down at the yuck and muck and mire all around your feet, or

Frame 2: You can look up, AND SEE THE SKY!"

The real dream teams that were studied in this project were clearly "looking up at the sky," keeping their eyes focused on the common mission.

The Mission Statement

One very practical tool many teams use to help focus their efforts is a mission statement. In addition to helping a team clarify its answer to the "why are we here" question, developing a mission statement also helps a team maintain focus during the daily routine as well as when major strategic decisions are made. The mission statement should be a short but powerful summary of the reason for the organization's existence. Developing a mission statement is a vital activity for community organizations, businesses, athletic teams, and other teams. Even some families have developed mission statements. The mission statement should be built around four key components: customers, key values, key players, and distinctive competencies.

For most organizational teams (businesses, governments, religious groups, volunteer groups), the key value is the customer or those that the team is formed to serve. Peter Drucker states time and again that the most fundamental mission of organizations is to *satisfy a customer's need*:

> A business...is defined by the want the customer satisfies when he buys a product or a service. *To satisfy a customer is the mission and purpose of every business* [emphasis added]. (Drucker, 1973, p. 79)

If one accepts Drucker's philosophy, then the starting point for mission formulation is to ask who is being served by the team. The answer to this question serves as the core of the mission statement.

A second component of the mission statement development process is the identification and clarification of key organizational values. What is really most important to this organization or team? Is it quality, safety, hard work, innovation, individual respect, profit, etc.? The mission statement development process can provide the opportunity to openly debate and clarify what the collective organization *really* values. Contradictions between words and actions become embarrassingly apparent. As a team identifies its core values, there is a tendency to want to compile a comprehensive list of all team values. The great team leaders who were interviewed for this book resisted this urge. Instead, they focus on and demand total commitment to the relatively few (usually three to five) values that are most critical to the success of their teams.

The third key component of mission statement development is the identification of the key players (in addition to the customers) required to achieve the mission. *Who* is going to be critical in the achievement of the mission—employees, stockholders, suppliers, etc.? An explicit identification and statement of who is important to the group provides the team with an even clearer sense of direction. Once again, the concept of *focus* emerges from the process of mission statement development.

The fourth key component in development of a mission statement involves identifying and making explicit the organization's area(s) of distinctive competence. What does this organization do especially well? Where do its competitive advantages lie? Consciously stating what have been assumed as implicit areas of distinctiveness helps to direct the organization's strategy toward the areas of its greatest strength.

The concept of a mission statement is not relevant only to new and existing organizations which have never been through the process; organizations with existing mission statements can be well served by the focus and sharp definitions that emerge from periodically examining the existing statement. Johnson and Johnson (J&J) conducts "mission challenge" sessions from time to time in which team members are encouraged to question the validity and relevance of the current statement. The consensus that emerges from these sessions creates a focus, oneness of mind, and unity of direction that allow organizations to pull together and react quickly in rapidly changing times.

When a disturbed person outside the J&J organization caused the Tylenol crisis by injecting cyanide into a few capsules, J&J was able to respond very quickly and decisively because of the clarity of its mission and values. A strongly embedded value in the J&J mission is the preeminence of customer safety and welfare. The clarity and widespread acceptance of this value caused J&J to ask, "What is in the best interest of our customers' safety?" and "How can we continue to deserve their trust?" The obvious answer was to recall all of the product that was on the retail market instead of just the isolated contaminated batch. This decisive action is thought to be largely responsible for building the customer trust and confidence that allowed J&J to quickly regain its previous market share once the crisis passed. Customers got the message—you can trust Johnson and Johnson!

THE TYSON FOODS MISSION STATEMENT

*"We are dedicated to
producing and marketing quality food products
that fit today's changing lifestyles."*

"We"—This word points to the family attitude and atmosphere that the company desires to create. It also reminds the "Tyson family" that their corporate culture de-emphasizes status and rank, that everyone deserves equal respect. The khaki uniforms that are worn throughout the organization—from the processing lines to the executive offices—are an example of the depth of meaning assigned to this one word.

"Are dedicated"—This suggests the level of commitment that team members should expect from each other. Nothing short of dedication is expected or acceptable.

"To producing and marketing"—This phrase identifies the key activities that create the greatest opportunities for success or failure in the organization.

"Quality"—This word is the foundation of all activities within the Tyson organization. It is the standard when evaluating the product, the package, the transportation system, selection of human resources, etc.

"Food products"—Although Tyson began as, and is still largely, a poultry-based company, the adoption of this phrase in the mission statement has already led to decisions that will ultimately result in the company becoming more diversified into other foods. Tyson already produces beef, pork, and seafood as well as flour and corn tortilla products in addition to poultry products.

"That meet today's changing lifestyles"—This phrase reveals what is probably the key element in the extremely successful Tyson strategy. While most of the company's competitors continued to process chickens in the traditional fashion (raw chicken or pieces of chicken in the meat case at the supermarket), Tyson Foods separated itself from its competition through "value-adding" activities. To Tyson, this meant activities such as deboning, precooking, breading, and creating fillets and nuggets. All of these activities add value to the product by making it easier to prepare and serve in a world of working couples, latchkey kids, frozen dinners, and microwave ovens. Not only are customers willing to pay more for this extra convenience, but they have also developed strong brand loyalty to this market leader. This strategy and focus, which are the Tyson mission, have played a large role in Tyson Foods being recognized by *Fortune* magazine as the most profitable company on the Fortune 500 list over the past ten years (1978–88). In a field where 12 to 15 percent return is a good number, Tyson has achieved an average annual return to shareholders of 52 percent. The Tyson experience suggests that a clear mission is related to the bottom line.

The Process Of Developing Mission

How a mission statement is developed is just as important as what a mission statement says. Several organizations were observed which had mission statements that had been formulated by the team manager alone. One organization even adopted a mission statement developed by an outside consultant. It is not particularly surprising that the existence of a mission statement seemed to make no difference in these cases. A manager in one of these organizations told us, "I'm really disappointed in my people. I worked hard on this statement and it's really a good one—they just don't seem to take any pride in our mission." This manager, along with many of us, needs to be reminded of a critical lesson about pride: you can't really be proud of something that you don't own. How many of us have ever washed and waxed a rental car and then stood back and admired it with a look of pride? On the other hand, almost all of us can remember the pride and care associated with the first automobile that we purchased. Why such pride and care? Because we *owned* it! So it is with mission statements—they must be owned by the team members.

A well-formulated, useful mission statement is the result of intensive discussion, negotiation, and collaboration among team members. The manager/leader is responsible for initiating and managing the process of mission development, but the entire team must accept responsibility for the actual mission. As the discussion/debate surrounding the development of the statement proceeds, the process will usually seem rather tedious. Intensive debate may surround just one word. Many groups have a tendency to minimize the conflict and say, "it's just a word, it doesn't matter that much." They are half right—it is just a word, but it *does* matter! The process of finding just the right words provides the clarification of values and the common sense of direction that make this such a valuable activity.

An incident observed at the Tyson Foods Management Development Center demonstrates the importance of words in this process. A team of managers from Tyson was having dinner in the food service area at the end of the first day of a two-and-half-day team-building session. The management development team, including the food service staff, had recently been through the session and had developed its own excellent mission statement, which the facilitators often used as a example for other groups. As Leslie, one of the servers in the food service area, poured coffee for one of the guests, she asked, "Have you guys worked on your mission statement yet?" "Well, yes, we have," was one participant's reply. Not yet satisfied, Leslie continued, "Did they show you our statement?" "As a matter of fact, they did use your team's statement as a positive example," was the answer. Leslie smiled and concluded, "Two words in that statement are mine!" The *pride* and *ownership* that this incident demonstrates explains why total involvement and consensual decision making are so critical to the process of mission development.

Writing or challenging a mission statement is often tedious, frustrating work. When we announce during team-building sessions that we are going to work on the development of a mission statement, it is not unusual for eyes to roll. Bob called his family together a few years ago to develop the Fisher Family Mission Statement. He explained that the purpose of the meeting was to begin a process to answer the question, "Why do we have a family?" Immediately all six eyes of his three teenagers rolled skyward, and comments such as "Please, give me a break" and "You've got to be kidding" flowed freely. But they stuck with the task and developed their own, very personal answer to the question. A few months later, Jennifer, who had been very annoyed when the process began, presented the family with a beautiful framed cross-stitch of the family's mission statement. That statement has helped guide the family through a variety of life experiences.

Is What You're Doing Important?

From a motivational point of view, creating a clear sense of mission seems to be *the most critical* leadership skill. Dr. Gertrude Elion shared the 1988 Nobel Prize in Medicine for her team's accomplishments, which included the development of two of the earliest active agents against leukemia. These and other advances by the team have been responsible for what some observers call a "revolution in chemotherapy." When visiting Dr. Elion at Burroughs Wellcome Company, where she has worked for over forty years, we observed how long and how hard the researchers there seemed to work. As leaders ourselves, we were amazed and asked her to tell us how she motivated the people to work so hard.

> I don't motivate them. All that I do is help them to see what is possible and to remind them of their responsibility to achieve that so that people can have a longer and better quality life. When someone new comes to work here, I sit down with them and talk about how important our work is. When we were focused on the leukemia research, I would tell them that there is a child out there who will die of leukemia today. There are others who will die tomorrow. There are some who will die next week, and some who will die next month until we find a cure. We've asked you to join our team because you and all the rest of us have the ability to solve this problem if we work long enough and hard enough. Once the team members catch a sense of that vision, I don't have any trouble getting people to work hard—in fact, I have more trouble getting them to take time off for themselves and their families!...We faced many medical problems and each was exciting and challenging.

We were amazed at her insight into the concept of mission, but we still weren't clear on the principle at work. We followed up by telling her we understood how she created such a strong sense of mission in her "life and death" situation and asking how could we instill a similar commitment in a less dramatic setting. Her response will remain unforgettable. "Is what your team is doing important?" she asked. "I guess so," one of us said. This sweet, kind woman suddenly became tough. "You guess so?" she asked incredulously. "I think I see the problem with the group you lead—your group has a leadership problem! You need to go away from here and think deeply about what you're doing with your life and decide if it's important. If you don't believe that what you're doing is important, then you need to get out of the way and let someone who believes lead."

The challenge facing every manager, parent, teacher, coach, and other leader is to think deeply about his or her organization and to lead the team in the creation of a similar sense of mission.

"A TURTLE ON A FENCEPOST"

PRACTICE #2:
MUTUAL SUPPORT, RESPECT, AND ENCOURAGEMENT

One life we got to do what we should.
One life, with each other, Sisters, Brothers.
One life, but we're not the same.
We get to carry each other, carry each other.

From "One" by U-2

It was in the area of support, respect, and encouragement that our real dream team leaders most distinguished themselves. This dimension of great teamwork is also the one that seemed to be most lacking in groups that emphasize traditional, authoritative approaches to making decisions and getting the job done. Whether we're talking about a family, a football team, a religious group, or a leading corporation, the ones that achieve greatness seem to be surrounded by an aura of support, respect, and encouragement.

We saw a video of a young, then-Captain Brady after concluding his first tour of duty in Vietnam. The reporter asked him how a "Dust-Off" pilot decided whether or not to go into a dangerous situation. Brady told him:

> Well, there's two schools of thought on that issue. One school says that I must consider the risks....I'm a highly trained professional, my crew is highly trained, and this helicopter is a very expensive piece of equipment and I have a responsibility to the U.S. taxpayers who purchased it—so I should not put all this at risk. The second school of thought says if that guy is down there in combat putting his butt on the line for me every day, then the *least* I can do is get him out if he gets hurt. That's my philosophy!

And in two tours of duty, Brady always went when called!

In discussing the importance of mutual support to team success, General Brady made a link between mutual support and the level of team motivation:

> The one thing that will make a soldier fight more than anything is the basic fundamental understanding that he will be cared for if he is hurt or that his family will be cared for if he's hurt—or that while he's gone they will be cared for and that his buddies will be cared for if they are hurt. This is the thing that drives soldiers to do so many incredible things that they will do in combat.

In the great teams we observed, people know they can trust and rely on each other, especially when they need each other. It is not unusual for people to support each other when things are going well. Most parents don't have any problem supporting their children when they make all "A's" or hit a home run. But it becomes much more difficult to support them when they get an "F" or strike out or get busted for drug use. Lou Holtz posed the dilemma best when he asked, "Why is it that when we need love the most, we deserve it the least?"

Think about the times in your life when you made mistakes and needed support. You can probably remember who supported you (and who didn't). And when they needed you, you were probably there for those people who supported you. One of the skills of great team leaders is their sensitivity to their team members' needs and their support for them when they are in need. If you want more support from your team members, then look for and take opportunities to support them.

It is very important to understand that supporting people does not mean that leaders never correct mistakes or do not instill discipline in their teams. In fact, the real dream team leaders we interviewed and observed did not overlook mistakes and view them as acceptable. A mistake was recognized and discussed in an appropriate manner, and what was appropriate depended upon the situation. Mistakes that resulted from not giving one's best were dealt with differently than those that occurred in spite of a person's best effort and good intentions.

After our interview with Coach Holtz, we attended a practice session of his Fighting Irish football team where we had the opportunity to observe how he applies this principle. The team was practicing a scenario that assumed Notre Dame was playing for the national championship, was behind by two points, had the football in their possession sixty yards from the goal line, and had no time-outs left with only two minutes remaining in the game. A well-oiled team went to work moving the ball down field according to the agreed-upon plan. With fifteen seconds remaining in the drill, the ball had been moved to within thirty yards of the goal line. The plan called for one more play—a down and out pass pattern that would take the ball out of bounds to stop the clock near the fifteen-yard line and set up what would be a relatively easy winning field goal. The receiver ran the pattern to perfection, turned, and the ball was in his hands. But instead of stepping out of bounds, the receiver noticed that the defender closest to him had slipped, so he cut to the middle of the field and headed for the goal line. Just as he appeared ready to score, a speedy defender appeared from nowhere and tackled him on the five-yard line. Time had expired and the "game" was over. All eyes focused on Coach Holtz as he charged down the field and grasped the jersey of the huge tight end who had made the mistake of not following the plan. "Congratulations," Holtz began, "you just cost Notre Dame the national championship! How does it feel to go down in history as the man who wanted to be the star of a national champion, but instead was the one who let all of his teammates, fans, and coaches down?"

Holtz's tough response to this mistake demonstrates that support is not a simple "soft" concept which says that "it's okay to just be average, don't worry about it." If greatness were that simple, many more would achieve it. The coach's judgment in this case was that the young player must learn the discipline that comes from trusting the knowledge and experience of his coaches and the efforts of his very capable teammates.

Later that same year, as we watched Notre Dame play the University of Miami in a game that would determine the national championship, millions of viewers had the opportunity to observe a different application of the same principle. Notre Dame was behind in the fourth quarter, and it began to look as if the Irish would lose the game and break their twenty-three-game winning streak. But then Notre Dame began to move the ball toward a touchdown that could give them an opportunity to win the game. Just as it appeared that they would score, a player made a mistake that gave possession of the football to Miami. We thought we knew what Lou Holtz's reaction would be. We watched with anticipation as the player approached Holtz on the sideline, only to be surprised to see Holtz give the player a hug, a pat on the rear, and an encouraging word. That's when we began to understand his principle. This player needed support much more than the player we observed in practice, and his mistake occurred in spite of his best efforts and good intentions.

Since this time, we have observed another interesting phenomenon about Lou Holtz's coaching style. He responds to his players' mistakes differently when his team is ahead than when it is behind. That's not really unusual; most coaches and other leaders respond differently. What is different is that Holtz seems to be tougher on his players when they are ahead than when they are behind! Most parents, coaches, managers, and other leaders do just the opposite. We believe Lou Holtz when he says he tries to love and support his players most when he believes they really need it instead of just when they deserve it.

Whether one is a parent, teacher, manager, or coach, dealing with mistakes is one of the toughest team leadership skills to master. Knowing when to support and encourage and knowing when to hang tough on discipline comes only from thoughtful experience. General Brady told us "...it's a trick. And that's why I say you can't care about soldiers or your children or anybody else and not correct them—even though it's a tough thing to do." Ignoring mistakes seems to invariably lead to mediocre or poor performance, but harsh responses can discourage.

The best a leader can hope for is to prepare the team for success and then have each team member do his or her best. When Bob's son, Rob, was in the third grade, he encountered a teacher/leader who didn't recognize the power of positively rewarding "good tries." One day, when Bob was passing through Rob's room, he found one of Rob's math papers (see next page). On this particular test, Rob had incorrectly answered five of the twenty problems. In fairness to Rob, it should be noted that he usually does much better, but he was apparently having "one of those days." In her wisdom, Ms. Woods, his teacher, had stamped a frowny face on his paper with the notation "poor work." Rob was not about to accept that evaluation

1. 42 ↙ Good werK
2. 52
3. 52
4. 81 ↙
5. 42
6. 63
7. 36.
8. 24
9. 33
10. 64
11. 72
12. 55.
13. 78
14. 24
15. 81
16. 21
17. 48 ✗
18. 26 ✗
19. 54 ✗
20. 62

Great!

I don't believe in having poor work, as long as I tried.

POOR I WORK

And I also don't believe in being SAD!!

sopace Pigwoods

To Mrs. Woods

Its You

Its You

of his work. First he tried to change the frown to a smile, but he wasn't satisfied with that. Then he drew his own smiley face and wrote "Good work, great!" Then he wrote the following two messages on the paper in an apparent attempt to counsel himself in regard to feeling a lack of support from his teacher: "I don't believe in having poor work, as long as I tried" (in reference to the "poor work" stamped on the paper) and "And I also don't believe in being SAD!!!" (in reference to the frowny face).

That's pretty good self-esteem and toughness for a nine-year-old. Unfortunately, not many adults or children have the courage to respond to criticism in this manner. How often have you worked hard and done your best, only to receive a "frowny face" from your leader? The common response to this type of criticism is to feel bad, incompetent, and unworthy. This nine-year-old's attitude further supports the theory that we are all born princes and princesses; our parents and teachers (and managers) turn us into toads. To prove he is human, Rob completed his "self-counseling" session by drawing two pigs—one a regular pig and the other a "space pig." He named them both in honor of his teacher!

At the foundation of mutual support and respect is our fundamental assumption concerning team members which we call the assumption of good intentions (see page 49). Most people want to do good work, are willing to work hard, and intend for their actions to contribute to the success of the team. Mentally healthy humans do not see themselves as evil or bad. Their behavior is rational, reasonable, and understandable *to them* most of the time. Even when their behavior appears to be negative (such as lazy, uncooperative, selfish, hurtful to others, etc.), people are usually just acting out their values and beliefs in response to their perceptions of situations. The challenge for the leader is to observe and listen to the messages from negative behaviors so they can come to *understand*. Once one understands, then, and only then, can a leader know how to respond.

A mother who actually comes to understand the why behind her teenage daughter's dysfunctional behavior is much better equipped to successfully relate to the daughter and to provide the love, nurturing, and support that are required to solve the problem. If a mother, manager, coach, or any other leader approaches a team member with an attitude that assumes bad intentions, then a defensive and negative response is highly likely. One of the most powerful dynamics in human relationships is that you get what you expect from others.

ASSUMPTION OF BAD INTENTIONS	ASSUMPTION OF GOOD INTENTIONS
People must be watched	People are capable of self-direction
People can't be trusted—they're not worth the risk	People are of ultimate worth; they are priceless and can be trusted
People won't work hard unless forced to	People are inherently motivated by a desire to do their best
People lack a sense of pride	People possess an inherent sense of pride when they share ownership
People will only perform well when they have to—under competition	Collaborative learning is a sustainable advantage
People only look out for self and not others—personal gain is the primary motivator	Given the right environment and the opportunity, people will choose collaboration which leads to the overall best
There is a winner and a loser in every conflict	"Win–win" solutions are usually possible as an outcome to conflict
The leader must be in control	The leader is willing to trust the capabilities of team members

---
OUTCOMES OF DIFFERENT ASSUMPTIONS

Expect mediocrity, get mediocrity	Expect the best, get the best
"Cover your hind-side" mentality	Trusting, supportive environment
Wasted energy	Energy directed toward mission
Defensive, blaming environment	Positive, problem-solving environment
Fail to achieve full potential	Know the joy of realizing full human potential

Encouragement is another important dimension of this practice of great teams. We must get over the idea that praise and recognition are extremely scarce resources which we may run out of if we're not careful. As an example, consider one management workshop that focused on increasing the level of praise within an organization. After several sessions, the supervisors were instructed to make a special effort during the week to try to find something to praise about each of the people they supervised. The workshop leader told them that each member of their team would be given a special wooden chip and would be instructed to give their supervisor the chip if he or she paid them a genuine compliment. The number of chips each supervisor brought to the next meeting would be an indicator of the effectiveness of the training. After the supervisors left, the workshop leader explained the concept to the workers. One person asked for clarification. "You mean if my boss says something nice to me I'm supposed to reach in my pocket and give him this wooden chip?" "Yes, that's it," replied the workshop leader. The worker replied, "Well, while you're at it, why don't you just give me two and then I'll have a lifetime supply!"

While this worker's comment may seem amusing and even sad, it could prove interesting to try the same approach with the people you encounter in your family, at work, in community organizations, and throughout your daily walk. How many wooden chips would you get in the course of a day? Many of us would be surprised at how we hoard compliments and praise, even though we often receive more in return for giving a compliment than we gave away!

This tendency to limit our praise of others can also be observed in the rarity of "thank-yous" in today's world. When someone is especially helpful, nothing can be more encouraging than a simple "thank you" from the team member receiving the help. Just how rare are "thank-yous" in today's environment? When we were on the Notre Dame campus to interview Lou Holtz, we stopped by the library and noticed that the office of Father Theodore Hesburgh, who was president of Notre Dame for thirty-five years, was located there. On the spur of the moment, we decided to drop by his office and try to meet this visionary leader. Much to our surprise and delight, we were able to arrange an appointment later in the day and were then able to spend an hour talking with Father Hesburgh, who recently retired after devoting his life to helping people. We asked him to tell us the most disappointing thing he had learned about people in his life's experience. After a thoughtful pause, this normally optimistic man frowned and said:

> The lack of appreciation from the people that I've supported and helped. When I was a young priest, I used to read the story about Jesus healing the ten lepers and had a hard time believing the response of the lepers. You know the story, the one where Jesus heals the ten lepers and they go away rejoicing, and then one returns to say thank you. I just had a hard time believing that—here are ten people whose life has been restored, their hope renewed, and only one

expressed true gratitude. After a lifetime of helping, supporting, and going out on a limb for other people, I've come to understand that Jesus had a pretty good average with one of ten!

Like praise, thank-yous don't cost much—just a little thoughtfulness and a genuine recognition that we never win alone. In any real success, there are always several people who are supportive and helpful, and who therefore deserve our sincere thanks. After thinking about what Father Hesburgh said, we have made it a practice to take about thirty minutes a week to think of one person who is deserving of a sincere thank-you and then write that person a brief note of thanks. People's responses to these notes have been extraordinary. They don't know what to think, but they sure like it! We really do have an unlimited supply of "warm fuzzies" (things we can say and do that make people feel good).

Probably the most fundamental principle in regard to mutual support and respect relates to the importance and value of people. The great team leaders communicate a message that people have ultimate value and worth. They display a "bone-deep" respect for every member of the team. They believe that because people are so important, they are worth the effort and risk the leader must put forth to support them. And because their belief in the value of people is bone deep, they don't have to contrive and fake superficial responses that represent only "skin-deep" support.

Tom Peters, the influential management writer and speaker, uses a story to demonstrate that the leader's respect for people must be genuine and cannot be faked. He tells of a company-wide banquet that was held to celebrate the best year in a firm's history. A huge convention hall was rented for the event. The supervisors, line workers, and their spouses were seated on the floor of the hall, while the divisional and "top" managers were seated on a stair-step series of risers that resembled the company's organizational chart—division managers on the first level, vice-presidents on the next level, and the company president and chairman of the board served as the "star" on this Christmas tree arrangement.

The seating arrangement alone provided a good clue as to the true philosophy that was driving this company. Then the company president began to speak. He first reviewed the year's successes and very humbly noted that he could not have achieved this success alone. Good start. He then continued by thanking each vice-president by name for his or her efforts and contributions to the company's success. He's doing even better and he should have stopped. But, as presidents tend to do, he went on too long. With a sweep of his hand toward the several hundred supervisors and line workers seated on the convention hall floor, he concluded, "And finally, a very special thank you to all of you 'little people' out there who made our success possible!" Little people? These people appeared to be pretty normal in their physical size. What was little about them? Apparently what was little about them was their value and the amount of respect that the president had for them.

This thinly disguised contempt for people who are willing to work hard for a living is the opposite of what we observed in the real dream team leaders. At Tyson Foods, almost everyone in the company—from production workers, to Buddy Wray (president and chief operating officer), to Leland Tollett (chairman and CEO), to Don Tyson (senior chairman of the board)—wears a khaki uniform at work. The uniforms are not just a gimmick; they serve as a constant reminder that "we are all on the same team and we must all do our best to be successful." The Tyson philosophy came through loud and clear during our interview with Don Tyson. In phrasing one of our questions, we used the word "employees." Tyson very firmly communicated to us that "we don't use that word in our company."

[Our philosophy] is really nothing but a people concept. I think that's the key word if you've got to...get
anything out of me—it's people working together. I
charge everybody twenty-five cents anymore if they
say the word "employee." That's a non-word in our
company anymore. You can say it as many times as
your want to, but it costs you twenty-five cents every
time.

This respect for people also shows up at Tyson in
what Don Tyson calls the "People Participation Plan." The
people at Tyson Foods all have the opportunity to purchase a number of shares of Tyson Foods stock and the
company will match their purchases by contributing fifty
cents on the dollar. The vast majority of Tyson people are
significant stockholders. Every week more than 26,000
Tyson team members allocate part of their paycheck to
the purchase of stock in the company. Don Tyson related
a remarkable example:

One of the greatest stories I've got—I hired this lady
twenty-eight years ago when I started the Springdale
plant. And so Judy worked with me all during that
time and I went to her retirement party, and we had
coffee and cake at lunch and we shut down the plant
for a while and we all visited about how long Judy
had been with us. But after the thing was over, she
came along and she said, "Don, I started on the stock
participation plan and I could only put in $5 a week
when I first started, but then I got up to $10 a week."
And she told me on that day she had $258,000 worth
of Tyson stock!

Emotional and psychological support is great, but for
a profit-oriented company, the concept of support wears
thin after a while if there is no financial support. Tyson
says, "Not only do our people work with us, they're part
of our family."

A willingness to share the fruits of the team's efforts

seemed to be common to all of these real dream team leaders. While these leaders were all exceptionally talented and highly motivated individuals, they all seemed to understand that their team's success is the result of the best efforts of every team member. When Gertrude Elion returned from Stockholm, Sweden, after receiving the Nobel Prize for Medicine, she called a meeting of her research team at Burroughs Wellcome Company. One of her co-workers told us she was rather surprised when Dr. Elion entered the room displaying the gold medal she had received as a part of the prize. This co-worker said that at first this appeared to be a somewhat arrogant act, and "this just wasn't like Trudy—she has always been such a humble person." The reason for the occasion and the medal soon became very apparent as Dr. Elion called for the attention of the entire group and asked her research team to line up around the room. She then approached the first team member and presented the medal to him. "The King and Queen of Sweden said to congratulate you— you've won the Nobel Prize!" Elion said. One by one, Dr. Elion communicated in a most powerful manner her deep respect and support for each of her team members. We were told that by the time she completed this process, "there wasn't a dry eye in the room." What a celebration!

When we talked with Dr. Elion, she said, "...since the Nobel Prize it's been very evident that all the people who contributed to these drugs all feel personally involved. They are walking on air. They are so happy for themselves, not just for me or for Dr. Hitchings. They feel part of it and they are part of it."

Donald Petersen, recently retired chairman and CEO at Ford Motor Company, is another great leader who understands the concept of mutual support, respect, and encouragement. As we were leaving his office in Detroit, we thanked him for his time and his willingness to share his insights. We complimented him on his leadership one more time. After all, under his leadership Ford Motor

Company had rebounded from the edge of disaster to once again become a thriving, highly competitive organization. Petersen seemed a little embarrassed and/or irritated by the compliment. He said, "I still don't think you understand what I've been telling you about my role at Ford—come back in here [motioning toward his office]— I want to show you something." There on the coffee table in his office was a rather unusual display encapsulated in glass. Inside the glass was a portion of an old wooden fencepost with a piece of barbed wire attached. Sitting on top of the fencepost was a crystal turtle. Petersen asked, "What do you see here?" The response was, "Well, it looks like a turtle on a fencepost." "That's right," Petersen said. "And if you ever see a turtle on a fencepost, you've got to know that he didn't get there by himself—he had a lot of help! If you want to write about me, that's O.K., but don't forget that the only reason that you're interested in talking to me is because of the recent success of Ford Motor Company. And that success is the result of the dedication of the 350,000 people who are Ford Motor Company— don't write about me without writing about them!"

"NONE OF US IS AS GOOD AS ALL OF US"

PRACTICE #3: CLEARLY DEFINED AND ACCEPTED ROLES

The crux of it is to motivate people to want to do what they most like to do. And if you find the right niche for each of the people on the team and you know that this is their expertise, they'll want to do it. And if they want to do it, they'll do it well.

Always help people see how they fit into the big picture. If you don't explain it, you're never going to get the same effort as you do when people know what they're doing, want to do it, feel part of the team, and feel like not just a cog in the wheel, but an *important cog* in the wheel.

Dr. Gertrude Elion

What Dr. Elion is telling us is at the heart of understanding one of the most mysterious concepts in life: What is it that motivates some people to exert incredible effort and show total commitment to the team while many others seek to get by on minimal commitment and effort? While hundreds of books and thousands of articles have been written in an attempt to explain numerous theories of human motivation, we believe that Dr. Elion captured the essence of understanding motivation in the preceding two paragraphs. What *really* motivates people is doing what they enjoy doing and knowing that they make a difference!

All of us want to know that we contribute and that our work counts for something—that we make a difference. The average person spends over half of his or her waking time, about 90,000 hours, on the job. We want this significant investment of time to matter. As parents, we devote thousands of hours to helping our children become independent, happy, productive, ethical contributors to society. We want to know that our efforts count for something. As community volunteers, whether we devote time to youth programs or organizations to help the homeless, we want to know that our investment of time and energy pays off. The most demotivating, dreaded outcome of any of these efforts would be to reach the conclusion that "No matter what I do, the results will be the same—I'm wasting my time." The ultimate expression of this negative attitude was embodied several years ago in the words of a song by the rock group Pink Floyd: "All in all, you're just another brick in the wall."

For a person to give his or her best effort, the specific role must be clear and the expectations that others have for that role must be understood and clearly communicated. In addition, people must know how their roles relate to the "big picture" or the overall mission. In short, each person needs to feel like an *"important cog in the wheel"* that leads to team success.

The essence of roles is that everyone on the team has a critical part to play if the team is to achieve its mission. The "star mentality" and the "hero myth," which have become so ingrained in American culture, no longer serve us well. The incredible individual feats of the Lone Ranger, Wonder Woman, Superman, and Batman are really unrealistically mythical in the reality of the new environment. In today's complex, sophisticated, highly interdependent world, none of us is likely to achieve anything of significance without a tremendous amount of help from others. From the White House to General Electric, we increasingly see top executive teams looking for ways to capitalize on the talents and intelligence of all team members. McDonald's Corporation's continuing success in the culturally diverse international marketplace is rooted in founder Ray Kroc's rejection of the "star mentality" which afflicts so many organizations and teams. His pivotal statement, "None of us is as good as all of us," is a call for all would-be winners in the twenty-first century to pay attention to each person, appreciate diversity, and build ownership.

The Disney organization captures the essence of individual roles as well as any organization. At a Disney theme park, all employees are "cast members." They are performers who are "on stage" when they come to work, and each role is critical to the Disney magic. The "Wiffle Dust" experience of millions of visitors per year is a combination of efforts that results in quality entertainment and fun in a polite and clean environment. One discourteous response, one dirty restroom, one unsightly area, just one cast member not playing his or her role and the magic is gone.

In the early stages of our interview with Steve Trent of the Thunderbirds, we talked about the five or six pilots who actually fly the planes as though they were the entire Thunderbird team. As the interview progressed, Trent made it clear that he was talking about something much bigger than the six pilots:

> Oh no, that's what the public sees, the six demo pilots and that's not my team....My team is 141 people.

They are all Thunderbirds. I don't allow them to call themselves "support personnel." They are Thunderbirds.

He went on to explain that the Thunderbird team includes the mechanics, the public relations people, the advance team, the people who make travel arrangements for the shows, and the numerous other people whose functions are required for a successful performance:

Today we've got officers and people from maintenance and administration at several radio and TV stations. One of our maintenance technicians [Scott Haynes] went to the Boys Club. Staff Sergeant Haynes is going to get some positive feedback from them that is going to hopefully make him feel good because the boys are going to ask, "How often do you travel? Do you like being a Thunderbird?" He is a Thunderbird...Staff Sergeant Haynes is a Thunderbird as much as I am a Thunderbird! We all wear the same patch, and after the show is over, we all sign autographs—pilots, mechanics, all of us.

Doesn't this type of attitude just make sense? If you were flying jets at 450 m.p.h., wings overlapped, eighteen inches apart, wouldn't you want to know that the mechanics and maintenance people felt that they were a part of your team? As a further indication of the total team concept, the pilot's name is emblazoned on the right side of the cockpit and the chief maintenance person's name is on the left side.

There is a powerful difference between "I'm just a maintenance person for the Thunderbirds" and "I'm a Thunderbird and I support the mission by doing my part." The difference between "just having a job" and having an important role in helping the team achieve its mission makes all the difference. Just a secretary, just a volunteer, just a supervisor, just a student, just an hourly employee—"just a job" carries zero passion and is extremely self-effacing. On real dream teams, there is no such thing as "just a job." Every person in every position can justifiably be proud.

Strength Through Diversity

When the Dallas Cowboys won the Super Bowl in 1993, we heard a lot about the performances of quarterback Troy Aikman and running back Emmitt Smith. They are certainly two great football players, but how many games would Dallas be expected to win if every player on the team was just like Troy Aikman or Emmitt Smith? Probably none, because these talented men are only competent at specialized roles. Dallas won because of the diversity of the team—different team members who are capable of playing different roles.

Coach Jody Conradt of the Lady Longhorns observed, "I think the best players I've seen are the ones who know themselves best and play within themselves and don't put themselves in a situation where their weaknesses are exposed. Everybody does what she does best."

Accepting the need for diversity of roles as well as the diverse skills and abilities of individual team members provides an interesting challenge for team members and team leaders. "Different strokes for different folks" sounded like a reasonable idea when Sly and the Family Stone sang about diversity in the 1960s hit "Everyday People." Unfortunately, there is ample evidence that most people have great difficulty respecting the diversity of other people's skills, values, and cultures. The most extreme expression of this failure is war, where people become so unaccepting and disrespectful of others that they want them dead. Other more common expressions of this problem occur when different departments in the same organization engage in win–lose competition or when a family member seeks to redefine a role as the result of change and/or personal growth.

"Different strokes for different folks" sounds great until it is applied to your daughter or son or spouse—then it takes some getting used to. But if you can genuinely appreciate the need for and the value of diversity in your team, then you have the potential to build a truly extraordinary team.

One of our greatest emotional surprises as parents has been the beautiful uniqueness of each of our children. Intellectually, from our backgrounds in psychology, we were well prepared for individual differences. But as the early childhood years unfolded, we found ourselves scrambling to fully value and appreciate the rich diversity embedded in our children. It was a continuous challenge for us to grow as parents. Our children demanded, often in quiet, persistent ways, to be recognized and heard. They seemed to be saying:

> My gifts are different. I will express myself and choose differently than you. My uniqueness is my strength. I feel your love for me, but your generation has not been kind to this planet nor to each other. There must be a better way. I am both scared and strong...Give me your love but not your plan. Listen. Support. Encourage. Trust.

We learned no more important lessons than these as parents and family members.

Michele Hunt is a member of the Herman Miller Company in Zeeland, Michigan, which has a global presence as a producer of high-quality, innovatively designed office furniture. Ms. Hunt believes that Herman Miller Company understands the value of diversity:

> The concept of diversity took precedence at Herman Miller because we recognized that we could never get

to high-performance participation without valuing the uniqueness that each person brought to the organization....We have discovered that the teams which work best together are those which have struggled together to appreciate each other. My uniqueness—which includes being a woman and African-American, and everything else that I am—is what I want to have valued. (*The Fifth Discipline Fieldbook*)

Wanting to be valued and wanting to make a difference are at the core of what motivates people. When teams capitalize on this rich human desire, Ray Kroc's "all of us" becomes quite powerful.

Personal Style Diversity

Research on the diversity of social styles has much to offer in helping to understand and accept diversity as a strength. Whether studying the work of Roger Reid and David Merrill at the TRACOM Corporation or the Myers-Briggs assessment, the underlying message is the same: we are all different and we need each other to accomplish the team's mission. Coach Jody Conradt of the Lady Long-horns used the Myers-Briggs assessment to help her players recognize and accept their different styles. "What I wanted them to get out of it was tolerance. I think athletes as a group aren't very tolerant of differences."

Conducting a style assessment with a team and discussing its implications can be a significant tool in helping people to work together. The basic message of social styles is summarized in the following points:

1. All people are different.

2. Each person has a "comfort zone" or preferred way of relating to others (style).

3. All styles are equally valuable to the team in leading to success.

4. Diversity of styles creates strength within the team.

5. Diversity of styles requires that each member of
   the team respect the style of others.

6. Team members are most successful in helping
   the team when they are versatile—that is, when
   they adapt their style to the situation and to the
   style of their teammates. The real test of versatility is the degree to which others perceive a person
   as being willing to accommodate the needs of
   others.

The TRACOM SOCIAL STYLES* Model identifies four
basic styles: Analytical, Amiable, Expressive, and Driving.
In reality, there are as many different social styles as
there are people, but the Reid and Merrill categorization
creates a general model that demonstrates the diversity of
people's style along two dimensions: assertiveness and
responsiveness to people. The SOCIAL STYLES Identification Chart summarizes the basic characteristics of each
of the four styles.

We've all had the experience of working with or living
with someone whose style is the opposite of ours. As
challenging as this can be, we often discover over time
that we become a pretty good team! For example, people
who behave analytically and expressively are opposites in
the TRACOM model, but they clearly need each other.
Expressives need Analyticals to slow them down, encourage rational thinking, and make them "look before they
leap." Conversely, Analyticals certainly need Expressives
to urge them to action, to help them sell ideas, and to
give them an emotional lift and encouragement.

---

* SOCIAL STYLES is a service mark of the TRACOM Corp. The SOCIAL
  STYLE Model is a trademark of the TRACOM Corp.

SOCIAL STYLES IDENTIFICATION

Analytical		*Driving*	
tends to be perceived as being:		*tends to be perceived as being:*	
+	−	+	−
Industrious	Critical	Strong Willed	Pushy
Persistent	Indecisive	Independent	Severe
Serious	Stuffy	Practical	Tough
Exacting	Picky	Decisive	Dominating
Orderly	Moralistic	Efficient	Harsh
Thinker		**Doer**	
Technical Specialist		Command Specialist	
Stress Reaction: Avoidance		Stress Reaction: Autocratic	
Amiable		*Expressive*	
tends to be perceived as being:		*tends to be perceived as being:*	
+	−	+	−
Supportive	Conforming	Ambitious	Manipulative
Respectful	Unsure	Stimulating	Excitable
Willing	Pliable	Enthusiastic	Undisciplined
Dependable	Dependent	Dramatic	Impulsive
Agreeable	Awkward	Friendly	Egotistical
Feeler		**Intuitor**	
Relationship Specialist		Social Recognition Specialist	
Stress Reaction: Compliance		Stress Reaction: Personal Attack	

The bottom line of SOCIAL STYLE diversity can be summarized in two points:

1. The most effective teams will be comprised of people with diverse styles.

2. When a team finds itself without diversity, individual team members need to be aware of the void created by the lack of diversity. They then need to demonstrate versatility when the situation requires it by flexing and shifting styles to fill the void.

If a marketing team finds itself planning a major advertising campaign with only Expressives on the team, one or some of them need to raise some analytical questions about the reality of budgets, time constraints, competition, and risks.

In reality, we all have the potential to act out each of the four styles. But to do so requires us to think, analyze situations, monitor our weaknesses, and develop a full range of social skills to match the needs of the situation. To flex into a style that is the opposite of your natural style feels awkward and uncomfortable, but with commitment and practice, a sense of skillfulness and confidence can be developed in our versatility.

Developing win–win solutions requires a lot of empathizing, inquiring, and seeking to understand, as well as a lot of self-disclosing and sharing. The teams that have committed to understanding themselves better, becoming sensitive to differences in style, and appreciating diversity have consistently found the process to be enlightening and empowering, both professionally and personally. They invariably report greater success in talking more openly about the formerly taboo areas of individual preferences and differences.

In a chaotic world of rapid change, intense competition, and limited resources, versatility is a most valuable trait of team members. A couple of years ago, Jose

SOCIAL STYLES VERSATILITY STRATEGY

	Analytical	Amiable	Driving	Expressive
Key Asset	Systematic	Supportive	Controlling	Energizing
Backup Behavior	Avoiding	Quiet	Autocratic	Attacking
Need To	Decide	Initiate	Listen	Check
Measure of Personal Value	Respect	Approval	Power	Recognition
Needs Climate That	Describes	Processes	Responds	Collaborates
Let Them Save	Face	Relationships	Time	Effort
Make Every Effort To Be	Accurate	Cooperative	Efficient	Interesting
Support Their	Principles	Relationships	Conclusions	Visions
Stress Benefits That Answer	How	Why	What	Who
Make Sure Recommendations	Process	Consensus	Options	Incentives
Follow-up With	Service	Support	Results	Attention

Oquendo of the St. Louis Cardinal baseball team demonstrated the ultimate in versatility for his team. Although Oquendo's regular role on the team was second baseman, the versatility of his skills allowed him to play all nine positions (including the highly specialized roles of catcher and pitcher) during one season.

Teams need Jose Oquendos. Organizations need people who are cross-trained so they can help out in other areas when they are needed. The recognition of this need has led to "pay for knowledge" systems in many organizations. Under this system, pay increments are earned by learning new skills and knowledge that make workers more versatile. Small businesses especially need versatile people to help them leverage their limited resources. Families need fathers who know how to "mother." And probably even more critical in American families, where more than 40 percent of children are being raised in single-parent households by mothers, families need mothers who are versatile enough to expand their roles to fill the void left by the absence of the father. The social costs of rigid, non-versatile parental roles are tremendous. Role shifting is certainly not an easy task, but achieving true excellence in teamwork has never been and never will be easy!

More Diversity: Organizational Applications

Dr. Norman Vincent Peale reminded us of the need for diversity in organizations in an unusual way. Using an organization that we often think of as homogeneous—the church—he reminded us of an organizational leadership lesson that was taught by the Apostle Paul to the church at Corinth. The shared values and beliefs of churches, synagogues, and other religious organizations form the core of their cohesiveness or ability to stick together. However, the mere existence of different roles seems to cause people to try to rank the value of roles. The people in the church at Corinth were no different. They had begun to debate among themselves as to which roles were most important. Paul instructed this young church of the need for diversity and the value of each role. Think about Paul's instruction to churches of all ages and you'll see why Dr. Peale suggested it as a blueprint for today's teams:

> There are different kinds of service to God, but it is the same Lord we are serving. There are many ways in which God works in our lives, but it is the same God who does the work in and through all of us who are His. The Holy Spirit displays God's power through each of us as a means of helping the entire church.
>
> To one person the Spirit gives the ability to give wise advice; someone else may be especially good at studying and teaching, and this is his gift from the same Spirit. He gives special faith to another, and to someone else the power to heal the sick. He gives power for doing miracles to some, and to others power to prophesy and preach. (vv. 5–10a)
>
> Our bodies have many parts, but the many parts make up only one body when they are all put together. So it is with the "body" of Christ (the church). (v. 12)
>
> Yes, the body has many parts, not just one part. If the foot says, "I am not a part of the body because I am not a hand," that does not make it any less a part of the body. And what would you think if you heard an ear say, "I am not part of the body because I am only an ear, and not an eye"? Would that make it any less a part of the body? Suppose the whole body were an eye, then how would you hear? Or if your whole body were just one big ear, how could you smell anything?
>
> But that isn't the way God has made us. He has made many parts for our bodies and has put each part just where he wants it.

What a strange thing a body would be if it had only one part! So he has made many parts, but still there is only one body. The eye can never say to the hand, "I don't need you." The head can't say to the feet, "I don't need you."

And some of the parts that seem weakest and least important are really the most necessary. Yes, we are especially glad to have some parts that seem rather odd! (vv. 14–23a)

So God has put the body together in such a way that extra honor and care are given to those parts that might otherwise seem less important. This makes for happiness among the parts, so that the parts have the same care for each other that they do for themselves. If one part suffers, all parts suffer with it, and if one part is honored, all the parts are glad. (vv. 24b–26)

I Corinthians, Chapter 12
The Living Bible, 1971

Coach John Wooden sounded somewhat like the Apostle Paul when he summarized how he built great UCLA basketball teams:

[I built teams] by defining roles for each individual and making each individual feel that their role is as important as any other role. Now there may be a lead role and then there's the supporting cast, but if you don't have the good supporting cast, the thing as a whole is going to fail.

Using this analogy of an automobile, the engine may be the most expensive and difficult to replace, but if you lose one little nut, the engine won't function. Now which part is more important? You've got four wheels, so if you lose one wheel, what good is the whole thing? I don't care how powerful the engine is or anything else, what good is it? So I tried to make each player feel that he had an important role. Some roles are going to be starters...who play most of the time. There will be other starters who will have people coming in for them. Then there will be players on the bench that seldom get in until the outcome has been decided. But they're playing a very important role toward the development of those who are playing the most in games.

Coach Wooden explained that if everyone does not accept their role and play it to the best of their ability, "the group as a whole is going to suffer."

Stars And Understudies

When the importance of every role is fully appreciated, the concept of team "stars" begins to lose its shine. Some of the most unappreciated team members are those who play the backup roles for other team members. The understudy actor in the play, the "scout team" in sports that mimics the next opponent in practice, and numerous other "on-call" roles are all equally important contributors to the success of a truly excellent team. Imagine arriving at the theater to find that twenty of the twenty-one cast members are prepared to perform, but the star is ill, so the play is canceled. Fortunately, this almost never happens, and it is at such times that we really appreciate the understudy who has been rehearsing faithfully for this moment. Great teams have great backups and understudies.

We actually encountered an example of this concept during our research for this book. We arrived right on time for our scheduled interview with Zubin Mehta, who at the time was the conductor of the New York Philharmonic. To our dismay, we were told that Mr. Mehta was ill and would not be able to lead the rehearsal we were scheduled to attend, nor would he be able to grant us the interview we had traveled so far to obtain. Carl Schiebler, the director of orchestra personnel, quickly stepped in and granted us an interview and arranged for us to speak with the substitute conductor. Our initial disappointment faded quickly as we realized that this situation had helped us more fully appreciate the importance of backup roles for great teams. We attended the rehearsal as scheduled, and this highly competent backup conductor led the orchestra in creating some of the most beautiful music we have ever experienced.

The Lady Longhorn basketball team of the mid-1980s provides another example of the importance of backup roles. During those years, the team featured two outstanding players at the position of center: Annette Smith and Cara Priddy. Smith, who may have been blessed with more natural ability, was the starter, and the hard-working Priddy played the backup role. It was generally accepted that Priddy would have been a starter for any other team in the conference, as well as for most teams in the country. Nevertheless, she played the backup role to Smith for several years. We saw a news report that included a sports interview with these two players. Priddy was asked how she felt about her backup role with the Lady Longhorns. Her response was quick and decisive: "I'd rather be playing a backup role on this team than be a starter on any other team!" Smith's comments indicated that she, better than anyone, appreciated the role Priddy played on the team: "The toughest competition that I face all year is going against Cara every day in practice. I'm a much better player because of her." Coach Conradt had an equally high estimation of Cara Priddy's value to their championship team:

> She was definitely a role player, a learned player. The rest of the team was very athletic with great natural ability. She was the kind of player who just practiced and practiced until she was a great shooter. She was not as quick and not as athletic as other players and she took a lot of abuse.

The value of having a totally committed backup player such as Cara Priddy was never more dramatically demonstrated than in the 1986 national championship game. The Lady Longhorns had compiled an unbelievable record of thirty-five wins with no losses, and only one barrier stood between them and their dream of a national championship—the University of Southern California team led by All-American Cheryl Miller. As the championship game progressed, Lady Longhorn fans watched in horror as Annette Smith, their star center, had to leave the game with a serious injury. At this critical point in the game, Coach Conradt sent backup Cara Priddy into the game.

> I never doubted that she was part of the glue that held that team together. And then suddenly, when Smith was injured, she came off the bench in the championship game and had a lifetime performance.

The Lady Longhorns won the game in grand style, and it was a total team effort that made their dream come true.

How Successful Leaders Utilize Roles

The great team leaders understand that every role is critical in order for a team to achieve greatness. They seem to follow a two-step pattern for fully utilizing roles:

1. They clearly define what they expect of each specialized role.

2. They then fully empower the person in each role and instill in them a sense that they are 100 percent responsible for accomplishing their assigned role with excellence.

Clear Role Definition

Clear roles mean that every team member fully understands the pattern of behavior that is expected of him or her. Each person knows how to contribute to the overall mission and how his or her role affects the efforts of every other team member. Misunderstandings and frustrations arise from lack of shared role definitions, which leads to fumbles, foul-ups, and important details slipping through the cracks. Comments like "I thought you were going to do that" are symptomatic of teams that lack clear role definition. Great teams simply do not have these types of misunderstandings on a recurring basis. If there is lack of clarity as to who does what, when, where, and how, the team talks about it until the difference is resolved. If performance levels are not clear between the leader and the team members, then the communication flows.

We heard about the need for clear roles time and time again from the team leaders we interviewed. Don Tyson explained the need for clear role definition and the importance of every role in a company that processes an enormous amount of food every week, including thirty million chickens:

> Without everybody in our company, I don't care what level they are, without them we don't have a company. Hey, have you ever tried to start Monday morning without that person cutting necks? I've got a real love for that person!

Coach John Wooden told us, "I think that one of my strengths was in getting players to accept their roles which I have clearly defined for them."

Carl Schiebler of the New York Philharmonic also said that clear role definition was critical for each member of the organization:

> ...in this organization...everybody has a job toward serving the art, whether you are selling tickets, raising funds, performing, promoting it, or whether you are involved in the operations. We all basically serve an art form. And we all play a part in creating an environment that is an artistic environment. So what

we have are the conditions that can make music, and make music well.

When organizations, families, community task forces, church or synagogue staffs, and other groups create conditions where people "can make music and make music well," extraordinary results are indeed possible.

Nowhere was the importance of role clarification and acceptance clearer than in the experience of General Brady: -

> We rescued 900,000 people during Vietnam. It was all done with teams—four people in each crew with distinct roles to play—the pilot, co-pilot, medic, and crew chief...We had a marvelous machine...and four highly skilled people who were faced with a bunch of obstacles—weather, terrain, enemy weapons, enemy locations, confined areas, just about everything that you can think of. You had to put all that together and you had to go in there and get that patient and get him to a hospital so that he could live. How? Each person knew his role and the role of other teammates. The mission was unquestionably clear and there was no way to reach it without each person playing his role well, time and time again.

The Brady story is a benchmark example for continually getting the best from everybody. When people have a valuable mission, know their part in helping realize the mission, and can trust each other for support, cooperation, and empowering communication, they can indeed overcome major obstacles and reach their mission.

Role Clarification And Negotiation

Whether at home, at work, or on the playing field, clearly defined roles are a major key to teamwork. One of the most useful tools for clarifying roles is a process we refer to as role negotiation. The role negotiation process involves two distinct steps. The first step is to identify dependencies. Who are the team members you depend upon the most in order to successfully play your part on the team? Why do you need them? Who needs you the most? The answers to these questions will tell you the areas of teamwork where clear roles are most important for team success. The second step in the process is to sit down in a one-on-one session with each person identified in the first step of the process and clarify what you do, what he or she does, and how you both can improve your teamwork. The communication in this session can be triggered by asking each person to:

- Provide the other person with a complete, detailed definition of my role on the team, as I see it

- Make a request of the other person for information, attitudes, and/or behaviors he or she could provide that would make me more successful in fulfilling my role

- Offer information, attitudes, and/or behaviors that I am willing to provide that would make the other person more successful in his or her role

This very simple, but rarely used, format for role clarification can produce some amazing "deals" between marriage partners, parents and children, and co-workers. In more than 80 percent of the cases we have observed, people are able to provide completely positive responses to the requests of the other person. In the other 20 percent of the cases, the deal may require additional negotiation or compromise. Very rarely (almost never) does this process not yield some positive results for the relationship and for teamwork. We have seen people who are supposed to be working together, but in fact are not, spend thirty minutes in this process and make a deal that resulted in hundreds of thousands of dollars in savings for their company.

This simple, straightforward process is a tool for harvesting potential win–win deals that are simply waiting to happen in most teams. The goal is to raise these types of issues before we get to the point where we ask our marriage partner, our parent or child, or our boss or coworker in frustration, "What do you expect of me?" The ultimate goal of utilizing this concept is to make the role negotiation process a standard operating procedure for your team so that the norm is to talk to each other frequently about these types of opportunities.

The "Litmus Test" For Clear Roles

From a conceptual standpoint, it is easy to see the importance of clear roles and each team member's keen awareness of his or her role and the roles of others. From a practical standpoint, however, the concept washes out quickly on most traditional teams. People simply cannot tell you the team mission or how role functions contribute to the mission, much less who the internal customers are. Team members pass the test if they can provide the following information regarding their roles:

- Tell me your primary role functions on this team. ("Do my job" is not an acceptable answer.)

- Which of your teammates are most dependent on you and why?

- On whom are you most dependent and why?

- What is the overall mission of your team?

- How do you contribute to the team mission?

It's a pretty straightforward test, but there is no way to pass the test quickly and comfortably unless you have taken time to think about these important issues. Most teams have not thought about either these issues or the implications for teamwork which logically follow. We invite you to do some "management by walking around" and some "naive listening." Wander around, ask the above questions to individuals at random, and listen carefully.

100 Percent Responsibility And Empowerment

Ensuring that each role on the team is clearly understood is the first step successful leaders take in utilizing roles, but clarity of roles is not enough. Successful team leaders must then fully empower each person in his or her role and instill a sense that each person is 100 percent responsible for accomplishing his or her assigned role.

It is absolutely critical that team leaders come to fully understand the empowerment issue. It has a lot to do with trust and support as well as individual competency, which are discussed in other chapters. But it also has to do with getting people to *accept* responsibility for their roles. It is not enough for leaders to simply say to team members, "You are empowered." Some managers struggle to help their teams understand that they really mean it when they tell their team members they are expected to make decisions and take action without waiting to be told what to do. It is not surprising that team members who have spent their lives in autocratic, hierarchical environments at home, at school, and at work have a hard time believing that managers really mean it when they say, "You're empowered."

One manager who successfully struggled with this process was Mike Hill of Alltel Information Services. We had been in several meetings with Mike and his team as he communicated and signaled the shift from a traditional, hierarchical mode of operation to an empowered team atmosphere. As the team gradually changed, it became apparent that not everyone was comfortable with being "empowered" or believed that Mike was really serious. While Mike seemed to recognize that empowerment would be a slow process, he became increasingly frustrated with the slow pace at which some team members were grasping responsibility. After offering empowerment to his team on several occasions, Mike decided to take a different approach and addressed his team as follows:

> Since I'm having a hard time defining and communicating what I mean by empowerment, I looked the word up in *Webster's* to see if there was a more direct way of communicating what I really mean. And there it was, after "giving authority to," after "delegating," and after "enabling others"—the fourth definition was what I was looking for. It was the legal application of the word empowerment—"...4. a legal responsibility." That's what I mean when I say you're empowered—it is your legal responsibility!

Mike Means, CEO at Arkla Gas, communicated this same message to the other leader/managers in his company: "I want quarterbacks who are willing to call their own plays."

Time and time again, we saw this attitude of 100 percent responsibility on the part of each individual comprising the great teams that we studied. Dean Sybil Mobley of the Florida A&M School of Business and Industry demonstrated this idea of 100 percent responsibility as clearly as any leader with whom we spoke. She has convinced the faculty, students, and administrators around her of what is possible and she does not allow any excuses for not accomplishing excellence. The whole approach at Florida A&M is a results orientation, one which says that trying hard is not enough. You can't quit until you get the results you are seeking. The inputs into the process or limited resources cannot be excuses for not accomplishing the goal. If the desired results are not being achieved, then the process should be adjusted and people will have to work even harder. The actual motto for the School of Business and Industry is, "No excuse is acceptable; no effort is adequate until effective."

The concept of 100 percent responsibility has the potential to revolutionize teams and team relationships. In fact, it has the potential to revolutionize many inter-personal, one-on-one relationships. Consider how often people who are having difficulty in relationships say something like, "If she would just meet me half-way" or "This relationship is going to have to be a fifty-fifty deal—me always giving more than I get is just not fair!" While we certainly understand the frustrations that these state-ments reflect and agree that taking equal responsibility for a relationship seems fair, we do not believe that a person is best served by entering a partnership or a team role with an attitude of partial responsibility.

What if every marriage partner, every parent, every son or daughter, every leader, every team member, every coach, and every player adopted an attitude of 100 per-cent responsibility for the success of the partnership or team? For example, what if both husband and wife accept 100 percent responsibility for their marriage relationship and their family? Contrast that with each accepting 50 percent of the responsibility. What if the husband, for whatever reason, slips to a 30 percent contribution? Even if the wife is still perfect and fulfills her 50 percent com-mitment, the relationship is only achieving 80 percent of its potential.

Truly great relationships and great teams are made up of people who are committed to accepting 100 percent responsibility for the team's success and are ready, will-ing, and able to do more than "their share" when neces-sary. This may be unfair at times, but if the cause is worthy, then unfairness may just be a part of the price of success. Even extraordinary teamwork cannot totally solve this reality. After all, life is not fair.

We heard a story about 100 percent responsibility from our friend Kevin Lee, whose brother participates in the Iditarod Trail dogsled race, a 1059-mile trek across Alaska each winter. While visiting his brother, Kevin observed that he had about seventy-five dogs when only eighteen are used to pull the sled. He asked his brother, "How do you choose the dogs you use in the race—what do you look for?" He expected some sophisticated answer that had to do with the genetic breeding, training, or at least certain physical characteristics of the dog. What he got instead was a very simple 100 percent responsibility statement: "I'm looking for a dog that will pull his weight!" Once again, attitude is equal to or more important than ability.

To demonstrate the 100 percent responsibility he tries to instill in his players at the University of Notre Dame, Lou Holtz tells the story of an event that occurred in 1898 prior to the Spanish-American War. The story, based on Elbert Hubbard's essay entitled "A Message to Garcia," is about getting a message from the President of the United States to the revolutionary general, Garcia, who was in the middle of Mexico and could only be reached by special courier. This was an extremely tough and dangerous assignment, but a very important one. A lieutenant by the name of Andrew S. Rowan was selected for the job and was dropped off by boat on one shore of Mexico. Three weeks later, after delivering the message to Garcia, he ended up on the other shore of Mexico. Lou Holtz has the following to say about this story:

> I'm not going to talk about the trials and tribulations of getting the message to Garcia (and they were great). I'm just going to say they ought to build a statue of Rowan on every college campus because he didn't ask, "Well, is it going to be hard?" "What do I get out of it?" "Who's going to help me?" "Where do I find him?" All he did was take a message and delivered it to Garcia.

And how difficult it is to find people today who will take a challenge, who will take responsibility, who will take an obligation without asking a million different questions and wanting everyone else to do it for them. If a guy is playing left guard and we call a play where he has to make an unusually difficult block and we call "take a message to Garcia," that's what we mean. Period. Just go get the sucker done!

"LET'S WIN CHAMPIONSHIPS"

PRACTICE #4:
WIN-WIN COOPERATION

Of all the characteristics of great teams, cooperation is one of the most difficult to define. Basically, cooperation is an attitude that is exhibited through behavior that seeks the common good. Attitudes are predispositions to respond to situations with a characteristic pattern of behavior. A cooperative attitude then would suggest that a person has made up his or her mind in advance to put the needs of the team ahead of any self-interest. A cooperative attitude is one that first asks, "What can I do for you?" instead of asking, "What can you do for me?"

A cooperative attitude is what Lew Alcindor (who later became Kareem Abdul-Jabbar) demonstrated during his days on UCLA's basketball team. In Alcindor's first year on the team, Coach John Wooden had a most telling conversation with him as he explained the options to his young star:

> I told him that we had two choices for the years that
> he would be playing for UCLA. First, I could design

an offense that would make him the greatest scorer in the history of college basketball. However, if we did this, we would probably not win any championships. The second choice was to use a strategy that would emphasize his rebounding, defense, shot-blocking, and passing as well as his scoring ability. With this approach I was confident that we could win championships, but Alcindor would not come close to the individual scoring record. When I presented him with these alternatives and asked him which he preferred, Alcindor said, "That's easy—let's win championships!" He was one of the most unselfish players that I ever coached.

The Potential For Win-Win

If this sounds strange, it's because this type of thinking and behaving is somewhat unusual, especially in the United States. The decade of the 1980s has been characterized by social scientists as the "me" years in the United States. The "me" tendency can be seen in the titles of several books that were popular in the 1980s, such as *Looking Out for Number One*, *Winning Through Intimidation*, and numerous other self-centered, self-help books. The emphasis was on getting what you want, however you can get it. Often that meant winning at the expense of others.

It remains to be seen whether the 1990s will become the "we" rather than the "me" decade. For this to happen, we will have to come to grips with two firmly entrenched thought patterns. The first is the strongly held U.S. cultural value of individualism. The United States was founded on the principle of individual freedom. Individual rights are emphasized over the role of government, which, in theory at least, is designed to seek the common good. While this intensely held cultural value of individual freedom is not necessarily incompatible with teamwork, intense national debate/discussion is needed to reach a clearer consensus as to how we define individual freedom in an increasingly interdependent world. While the Lone Ranger is often pointed to as glorifying individual effort, you don't have to watch many episodes of his adventures to figure out how short the series would have been without his trusty companion Tonto and his faithful horse Silver. The truth is clear—we need other people. We always have and we always will.

The prophet shares the following wisdom in The Book of Ecclesiastes 4:9-12:

> Two are better than one because they have a good return for their labor. For if either of them falls, the one will lift up his companion. But woe to the one who falls when there is not another to lift him up. Furthermore, if two lie down together they keep warm, but how can one be warm alone? And if one can overpower him who is alone, two can resist him. A cord of three strands is not quickly torn apart.

As the world continues to increase in complexity and interdependence, this ancient wisdom has never been more relevant.

The second thought pattern that inhibits cooperation is even more difficult to change because it is probably the most basic human instinct of all—self-interest. This is one subject on which psychologists, religious experts, philosophers, and academics all seem to agree: it is human nature to seek one's own self-interest. In fact, this is such a strongly held human instinct that we have no illusions about our ability to change it. We do, however, have some suggestions about how self-interest can be expressed in a more cooperative manner. In a complex world where we can't accomplish much by ourselves, it is usually in a person's long-term best interest to cooperate with teammates. Conventional thinking about self or other orientation has incorrectly been described as an either/

or choice. That is, our behavior can be classified as tending to be either self-oriented or other–oriented and the two are at opposite ends of a continuum.

Self-Oriented ←——————→ Other-Oriented

Cooperative choices can be expressed more accurately in the form of a two-dimensional graph, such as the following:

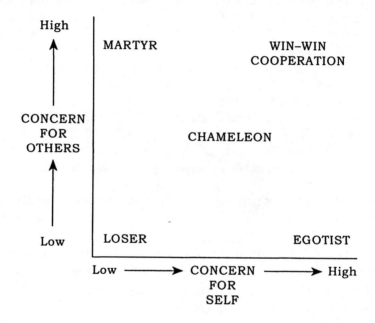

"We Have Met The Enemy"

When we adapt our thinking to this mode, then the potential for what we call true "win–win cooperation" becomes possible. The greatest problem with this type of thinking is overcoming the notion that we must compete with the people on our own team and create win–lose situations. Winning and losing are part of life, but the real challenge is in how we define winning and who we identify as the enemy/competition. Think about teachers you have known who define the enemy as their students, or managers who view their workers as adversaries, or organizations where one department considers another as the competition. Even some parents talk as if their own children were against them! Once again, "We have met the enemy and he is us!"

We must do a better job of defining the enemy or competition. Competitiveness is not a bad personal trait. In fact, it is highly desirable in a world filled with other groups, organizations, and teams that are often seeking the same scarce resources as your team. However, when one department (or one family member or, for that matter, any member of one team) seeks to win at the expense of another, then the team will be the worse for it.

If you were to take the time to evaluate the relationships in the variety of teams on which you work, play, and live, how many win–lose situations could you identify within those teams? Think about budget meetings at work or family discussions about household responsibilities. A thoughtful and sensitive look around would allow most people to identify plenty of win–lose competition going on between/among people on the same team.

How then do we change destructive intra-team competitive behavior into win–win cooperative behavior? The steps outlined below provide a framework for the necessary shift.

Moving From Win–Lose To Win–Win

1. Create awareness—To begin the change, someone must become aware that a win–lose situation exists. In some cases, the problem may be obvious to everyone involved, but in many cases people may think that they are winning when they are actually losing (win the battle but lose the war). Team leaders should be constantly alert and seek to identify win–lose situations and systems within their teams, and every team member should be encouraged to identify win–lose situations. The person most likely to be aware of a win–lose relationship is the loser—the winner often thinks things are going great!

2. Call it—The second step in moving from win–lose to win–win cooperation is for someone to raise the issue for discussion. A special challenge is that in traditional organizations, the loser is most likely the person who has less authority, rank, or power. In families, that means children (not parents); on athletic teams, players (not coaches); at school, students (not teachers/administrators); and at work, team members (not managers). For these less powerful people to raise win–lose discussions with their leaders requires genuine assertiveness and, sometimes, significant courage. But if teamwork is to be enhanced, someone must call it!

People are often aware of a win–lose conflict but avoid calling it in an attempt to keep from harming the relationship. Over time, this avoidance response causes people to build up resentment, anger, and overall bad feelings toward that person or persons as the situation gets worse and worse. The real irony here is that in a desperate attempt to save the relationship through avoidance, it is actually destroyed because of the accumulated bad feelings. Win–lose situations must be assertively and courageously addressed for a team to achieve its potential.

3. Negotiate for a win–win—The negotiation should begin with a focus on the common mission and how the current conflict prevents the team from reaching its potential. What often happens is that people begin the conflict resolution process by discussing/negotiating alternative solutions *before* clearly defining the issue or problem. If the parties will spend considerable time defining the problem in terms of the *needs* of both parties, then this well-defined problem is at least half solved.

A classic example of how the process can work is routinely played out at the dinner table of a family with young children. The dinner is going just fine until some well-intentioned parent, let's say the father, notices that Billy is not eating his boiled spinach. "Billy, eat your spinach," the father commands, without even realizing he has just created a win–lose confrontation. At this point, several scenarios become possible. Billy may just say, "Okay," and gulp down the spinach, which is unlikely. But if he does, then his father wins and Billy loses.

More likely, Billy could look his father squarely in the eyes and express an emphatic, "No!" Now we have a bigger problem with much higher stakes because the rest of the family is suddenly intensely interested in the outcome of this previously trivial conflict. If the father says, "Okay, just forget it," he loses, Billy wins, and the father may soon find himself buying a new car for Billy's teenage sister who now decides to ignore her curfew. Another possibility is for Billy to say, "Okay, I'll eat the spinach, but if I do I'll throw up." If this scenario is played out, the father loses, Billy loses, and everyone else around the table loses. The most common strategy that usually evolves at this point is one of compromise, where the father takes Billy's plate and moves a portion of the spinach to one side and says, "Okay, you only have to eat this much." If this still doesn't work, the final fallback strategy, in an attempt to save some face, might be "Okay, just take one bite." If either of these approaches works, then both Billy and his father win some and lose some.

Dealing with situations such as this would not be so bad if they just occurred once and then, no matter how poorly we handled them, we were through with them for good. But what is so frustrating is that it is not unusual for the same situation to occur and to be handled poorly repeatedly.

How could the win–win approach be applied here? It would begin with defining the problem in terms of the *needs* of both Billy and his father. How can we know their needs in this situation? We could start by asking them. If the father were asked, "What do you need from this situation?" he would likely reply something to the effect that "I want Billy to eat good nutritious food that will make him strong and healthy." If Billy were asked the same question, he would probably reply, "I want to eat food that tastes good." The win–win approach then combines the two sets of needs to define the problem as the need for the family to be served nutritious food that will promote their health and also taste good, or is at least acceptable, to everyone at the table. With the problem defined, the alternatives begin to flow—broccoli, brussels sprouts, asparagus, turnip greens, cauliflower, etc. Maybe nobody in the family actually likes cooked spinach, but they all like raw spinach served as a salad, and raw spinach is even more nutritious than cooked spinach. Talk about a win–win solution!

You might ask, "So your solution to the problem is to throw the cooked spinach away and go get some fresh, raw spinach and make a salad?" Probably not for that one incident at that one meal; after all, some degree of compromise may be necessary for the immediate problem. But what is so senseless is that the same win–lose confrontations take place over and over again, and the result is that everyone loses repeatedly. Following the prescribed three-step process outlined here has the potential to turn many typical win–lose situations into win–win success stories.

The Reality Of Conflict

Differences and conflicts in teams are expected and normal. We don't know of *any* team—family, work, athletic, community volunteers, church or synagogue—that never has any conflict. Conflict is normal, expected, and inevitable. The issue then is not how we avoid conflict or whose fault it is, but rather how to deal with conflict when it arises.

The results of conflict can be positive or negative. Some of the positive outcomes include generating new ideas, providing for more information exchange, clarifying important issues, increasing the energy level of the team, and reaching a better decision because alternatives were considered. When conflict is handled poorly and is routinely turned into a win–lose confrontation, then negative outcomes such as hurt feelings, poor decisions, disrupted communication, and distance between people are realized.

Cooperation does not mean that we don't disagree or discuss alternatives. Critical thinking is absolutely essential for teams in the decision-making process. However, it is not that unusual for leaders to respond to members who challenge methods, ideas, and processes by misusing team concepts and saying something like, "You are a team player, aren't you?" This direct attempt to reduce critical thinking has been identified as a common characteristic of "groupthink," a concept set forth by Dr. Irving Janis.

Janis describes how the phenomenon of groupthink played an unfortunate role in the infamous Bay of Pigs invasion during John F. Kennedy's presidency in the early 1960s. Some of Kennedy's advisors who were present during the discussions that led to the ill-fated decision to support an invasion aimed at overthrowing Fidel Castro's Cuban government have reported they had grave reservations about the plan, but they failed to express them in the meeting preceding the attempted invasion. It is reported that Kennedy and a few other key leaders in the group strongly supported the invasion. The failure of the opponents of the plan to speak up has been attributed to their desire to maintain the cohesion of the team and to be supportive of their leader. Interestingly, the tendency to suppress critical thinking and discussion (groupthink) is more likely to occur in highly cohesive groups where people really want to "stick together" and "get along." History shows the Bay of Pigs invasion to be one of the most illogical, poorly planned military actions that the United States has supported.

Contrast the Bay of Pigs decision with the decision that Kennedy and his advisors made during the Cuban missile crisis. When the United States discovered that the Soviet Union had positioned missiles armed with nuclear warheads in Cuba, just a few miles and minutes away from major U.S. population centers, Kennedy assembled his top advisors to consider a course of action. Being careful not to bias the members of the group with his opinions, it is reported that Kennedy began the meeting by giving a broad overview of the situation which included the facts and a definition of the problem. He then spent most of his time listening and asking clarifying questions. It is reported that he even deliberately absented himself from significant portions of the discussions so his advisors could openly discuss all of the options without being concerned about pleasing him.

Kennedy and his group then reached a consensus on a very tough, hard-nosed course of action some historians see as a turning point in the Cold War. The United State demanded that the Soviet Union immediately withdraw the missiles and enacted a naval blockade of Cuba to enforce that demand. The Soviet Union blinked, backed down, and withdrew the weapons.

Although both situations involved most of the same people, the Cuban missile crisis, in contrast to the Bay of Pigs, is often cited as a model of effective decision making. The major difference between these two situations can be found simply in the process that was used to reach the decision. In one case, the process repressed critical thinking and honest, direct assessment of the problem. In the other case, the process encouraged critical thinking/discussion and a direct honest assessment of the problem.

Even though it involved considerable disagreement and hot debate, the Cuban missile crisis model is the one to be emulated by teams that strive to reach their potential. Remember, a team player is not necessarily a "yes person." It could well be that the person who engages in the most critical thinking is the best team player and cares most deeply about the overall good of the team.

Learning About Win–Win Cooperation

The United States faces serious problems in building cooperation and a spirit of teamwork among students, parents, administrators, and the community as we attempt to prepare young people to successfully compete in an increasingly competitive world economy. Our educational system really has not done a very good job of preparing young people for a world that requires cooperative efforts. Remember how hard your teachers worked to prevent cooperative efforts when tests were administered!

One fifth-grade teacher knew one of her students was cooperating too closely with another classmate. The two students, who sat side by side, turned in identical answers test after test, but the teacher couldn't prove they were cheating and she couldn't be sure who was copying from whom. Finally, one of the students inadvertently provided the evidence the teacher needed to deal with this case of over-cooperation. The better prepared of the two students encountered a particularly difficult question that stumped her. When the teacher examined the responses to this question, she had the evidence she needed to prove her case. The better-prepared student responded to the tough question with a simple, honest, "I don't know." The boy sitting next to her responded with a double confession: "I don't know *either!*"

The education system is on target in requiring individual competence and knowledge on the part of every
student, but the system has failed in helping students
learn how to work together cooperatively. An increasing
number of schools are requiring students to work together in teams. Sybil Mobley and her team in the School
of Industry and Commerce at Florida A&M are on track
in developing college students to assume responsibility
and to develop their team leadership skills. At Florida
A&M, students are assigned to task-oriented teams when
they arrive as freshmen and continue to serve on various
teams throughout their stay at the university.

Another example of a team-oriented educational strategy comes from Perritt Primary School (grades K-3) in the
small town of Arkadelphia, Arkansas. We had heard a lot
about the school (it had received a presidential award as
a "National School of Excellence") and thought it would
be a good place to take an industrial prospect who was
considering locating a major industrial facility in the community. We called the principal, Wanda O'Quinn, and
made an appointment to take a tour of the school.

When we arrived, we were immediately impressed by
the environment—clean, bright, and positive. Ms. O'Quinn
greeted us and then introduced us to a couple of eight-
year-olds, Brad Butler and Laura Phelan, who were the
president and vice-president of the student body. She
then asked us to stop by her office again before we left
and began to walk away. We excused ourselves from our
guests and the two students and caught up with Wanda
to ask her if there was any way she could find the time
to accompany us on the tour. After all, our guests were
important industrial prospects and the tour was a pretty
big deal to them. She was very polite but firm in her
reply. We weren't so sure that turning this important tour
over to a couple of second graders was such a good idea,
but we apparently had no choice. "School tours are a
student responsibility. Laura and Brad will do a fine job,"
she informed us.

As we began the tour, Laura and Brad showed us a vegetable garden the students cultivate. At harvest, a meal is prepared in the cafeteria strictly from the fruits of their labor. They showed us pictures of their principal milking a cow in front of the school because the students had met their goal of reading a large number of library books. They showed us the artwork done by the five-year-olds in the kindergarten classes and posted outside their classrooms. "These are really quite good—they've worked hard and we're really proud of them," commented Brad. "You have to remember they're just in kindergarten," the "much older" second-grader added. They took us by Gwen Fullen's music room and told us of the recognition the music program had brought to the school. The third-grade "Nickelodeon Choir" had been the opening act at "America's Reunion on the Mall" celebration to kick off the activities at the Clinton inauguration.

Then they took us through the cafeteria, where the room was decorated and the lights were dimmed. "We're having a candlelight dinner today at lunch to honor our bus drivers. They help a lot of us get to school every day," Brad reported. We were amazed. After all, we had ridden school buses before, and we knew what most school bus drivers get for their efforts—and it's not a candlelight appreciation luncheon! We asked one of the bus drivers what he thought about all of this.

> I deliver kids to four different schools every day. I love these Perritt kids! If they aren't out by the road when I arrive in the morning I'll honk my horn and wait a minute for them. These brats from these other schools, hey, if they're not ready, it's not my fault. I don't even slow down.

The most telling incident of the tour occurred as we first entered the cafeteria. Near the door was a spot where a student had apparently spilled some milk. We noticed the spill, but just walked around. Without commenting to us, Brad asked Laura to take over our tour and excused himself from the group. We kept our eyes on Brad as we walked to the other side of the cafeteria. To our amazement, he went directly to a utility closet, took out a mop, cleaned up the spill, returned the mop to the closet, and rejoined our tour without any reference to the incident. It was at that point we realized the genius of the Perritt system. The cooperative attitude and sense of pride we observed in Brad, Laura, and other Perritt students were a direct result of a system that involves the students to such a degree that it becomes "their school." This level of ownership parallels what Don Tyson told us he was seeking from the people at Tyson Foods:

> If you see a job that needs to be done, don't ask, "Whose job is it?" It's your job. You're the one who's identified the problem and who sees the need for action. Just do it!

Don Tyson would do well to get a list of the alumni of Perritt Primary School to guide his company's hiring decisions. As you might expect, our industrial prospect was more than impressed with the tour, especially since the company planned to implement a self-directed work force in the new facility. We thanked Wanda O'Quinn for arranging the tour and for the commitment to developing people that she and the faculty of Perritt demonstrated. We now even had the insight to thank her for not going along on the tour!

Aligning Systems With The Cooperative Philosophy

To promote a cooperative team spirit, many teams need to examine the systems that control their day-to-day activities. For example, one of the reasons many business organizations do not get the desired levels of cooperation is that their systems do not encourage and support cooperative behaviors.

Performance evaluation systems in most organizations have traditionally rewarded individuals for star performance. An individual's career advancement has depended on the accomplishment of individual goals within the organization. The impact of evaluation/performance appraisal systems on team spirit was powerfully demonstrated in a team-building session we conducted a few years ago. The group consisted of a seven-member management team from a plant that was a division of a huge Fortune 50 company. At one point during the session, the discussion focused on the company's evaluation system. While all of the six department leaders were accountable to the plant manager, their career advancement was more closely tied to the evaluation of their performance by their counterparts at the corporate level—the plant controller was evaluated by the corporate controller, the plant industrial engineer was evaluated by the corporate industrial engineer, etc.

As the discussion continued, one of the participants raised a very interesting question. "If we were evaluated *only* on team operating results, and not as individuals, do you think that we would do anything differently—would it affect our decisions?" After some thoughtful discussion, all seven team members agreed that such a change would cause them to do some things substantially differently. Then one of the members blurted out a question that caused a deafening silence to settle over the group. "Well, do we want to do it? Should we ask corporate to evaluate us only on team results and not as individuals?"

Our knowledge of the performance of each team member was especially helpful at this point. We knew that among the seven members were two stars, one above average performer, three average performers, and one person whose performance was so poor that he was actually in danger of losing his position. The drama continued to unfold as all seven participants sat quietly for what seemed to be an eternity but was actually about two minutes. Finally, one of the team stars looked up and announced, "I'm willing to do it!" The other star gave him a startled glance, hesitated, and then said slowly but firmly, "So am I." One by one, the team members expressed their willingness to ask corporate to change to a team-based performance appraisal system. Only the poor performer had not spoken. When he finally spoke, his eyes were moist as he looked at each of his teammates and simply said, "Thank you."

For the next few months, he was on the receiving end of more help from his teammates than he had imagined possible. Suddenly, all of the members were acutely aware that the only way for them to win was to ensure that every one of the other team members won. This new organizational system, which now supported "win–win" team spirit, resulted in this plant becoming the low-cost, high-quality leader in this huge corporation. Together they achieved what John Wooden would describe as true *competitive greatness.*

Taking Win–Win To The Top Of The World

As discussed earlier in this chapter, cooperation is an attitude, and attitudes are predispositions to act. A person with a cooperative attitude has made up his or her mind *in advance* to put the needs of the team ahead of any self-interest.

The best example of this attitude was displayed by Lou Whittaker's Mt. Everest team. After months of grueling effort, five members of the team finally reached the final campsite at 27,000 feet. As they met in the crowded tent, with cameras rolling to record the event for PBS, it was time for Lou to make a critical and difficult decision.

With 2000 feet to go, it was time to make role assignments for the final assault, which would come the next day.

As one would expect, all five of these great climbers were highly motivated to stand at the summit of Mt. Everest—the top of the world. The first role assignment was easy enough. As leader, Lou Whittaker would remain at the camp to coordinate the activities of the team. When I asked him why he didn't go to the top of Everest, his answer was a classic for truly understanding leadership: "...Of course I didn't go to the top. It's my job to put other people on top!"

The other assignments were more difficult. Two of the remaining climbers needed to go back down to the previous camp; load up with additional food, water, and oxygen; and then climb back to the 27,000-foot camp. If they survived this support assignment, they would certainly not be in any condition to go for the summit. The remaining two members were to stay in the tent, eat, drink, breathe oxygen, rest, and then go for the summit the next day.

It is especially interesting to note the criteria for assigning roles at this point. What assignment are the two strongest climbers given? The toughest assignment is actually the support role of returning to the previous camp and ferrying supplies to the final camp, and this role goes to the two strongest climbers. The two weakest climbers rest, renew their strength, and receive the "glory" of the summit. To further complicate Whittaker's decision, one of the five climbers was Lou's son Peter. "It was tough. I knew it was Peter's dream to stand at the summit of Everest. But I also knew that Peter was my strongest climber at this point."

As the video cameras continued to roll, Lou paused for a moment, looked at his son, and then said, "Peter, you support." With only the slightest hesitation, Peter responded, "Okay." And that was it! No whining. No complaining. No "Why do you always pick on me?" Just "Okay."

Without a predisposition to do what is best for the team—a cooperative attitude—the team would have no realistic chance of achieving its goal of climbing Mt. Everest. But with that kind of cooperative attitude, the team put two people on the top of the mountain the next day. As Lou Whittaker explained, "If one person on our team makes it to the summit, then we have achieved our mission and we have all been to the top!"

"WHOSE ROPE
ARE YOU WILLING
TO HOOK INTO?"

PRACTICE #5:
INDIVIDUAL COMPETENCY

Leaders sometimes lament the fact that they can't lead
their teams to greatness because their team members
simply lack the skill or ability. The manager who says,
"You just can't get good people anymore" or the parent
who says, "I would trust my teenage son to decide, but I
just don't think he has the necessary judgment" seems to
have forgotten that the essence of leadership lies in developing people. If team members lack the ability or
judgment to perform at the desired level, then the leader
is responsible for providing the experience and training to
develop the individuals.

A couple of years ago, Bob invited Dr. Sybil Mobley,
Dean of the School of Industry and Commerce at Florida
A&M University, to serve as a Distinguished Visiting Professor at his university. He was not really prepared for
her response. Dr. Mobley said she could come and de-

scribe Florida A&M's outstanding program, but that she would very much prefer to send Dr. Bob Atkinson, one of her department chairs. The decision was made to defer to Dr. Mobley's judgment and Dr. Atkinson was invited. He did an outstanding job as a visiting professor, but all of the great "Sybil stories" he told only made Bob more determined to bring Dr. Mobley to his campus. When Dr. Mobley was invited the next year, she once again tried to send one of her other team members, but Bob finally convinced her to personally accept the assignment.

During her interview for this book, she made a statement that helped to explain why it was so difficult to get her to personally accept the assignment:

> My job is to develop people. It is my responsibility to provide my people with the development opportunities that they need to grow. The ultimate test of my ability as a leader will come when I retire in the next few years. At that time I'm going to ask myself, "Will my team miss me when I'm gone?" If the answer is yes, then I've failed!

General Brady expressed the same attitude, though in a different way, when someone asked him if military leaders aren't too valuable and important to risk their lives in combat situations.

> If he's a really good leader and if he's done his job and he gets killed, then he will have left behind a mechanism that will go on without him. If he can walk away and the organization does not miss him, then he's done his job. If he is not doing his job of developing people, and he is killed, then the organization is better off without him.

Many leaders seem to lack the self-assurance that General Brady and Dr. Mobley's attitudes suggest. Perhaps part of the problem arises because so many leaders become leaders because of their own extraordinary competence as team members—they have always been the "star." The transition these people find so difficult is moving from seeing themselves as the star to seeing themselves as the leader whose job it is to make stars out of other people. Dr. Sybil Mobley, General Brady, and the other real dream team leaders understand that leaders should develop people to the extent that they can. In the words of Rosabeth Kanter (*The Change Masters*), leaders should "make everyone a hero."

That attitude of making heroes of others was clearly evident in our conversation with mountaineer Lou Whittaker, the first to lead an American team to the summit of Mt. Everest. When we asked Whittaker to identify his "greatest team experience," he immediately said, "It was when we climbed Everest in 1984." We followed up by asking, "So you have climbed Everest?" Whittaker simply responded with an affirmative nod. We knew he was the leader of the team that climbed Everest, but we didn't think he was one of the two climbers who had actually stood at the 29,000+-foot summit, so we followed up again. "So, you have been to the top of Everest?" we asked. Whittaker looked a bit puzzled and then responded, "That's right." We pressed a little further in an attempt to make a point by asking, "Then you have personally been to the top—your feet have stood at the summit of the tallest mountain in the world?" For the only time during the interview, Whittaker appeared irritated: "If you want to know if my feet have stood at the summit, then the answer is of course not! The leader never goes to the top!"

Lou Whittaker went on to explain that the leader's job is to stay at the final camp and make important decisions about supplies, personnel, safety, strategy, etc. It is not the leader's job to always be in the "spotlight." Many of the leaders we have observed seem to have trouble accepting the role of the leader as servant over the role of the leader as king. However, the real dream team leaders we interviewed seemed to have a deep understanding that their success as a leader is totally dependent upon the effort and ability of each of their individual team members. How, then, do they encourage the effort that is required to develop personal excellence in each team member? Where do they start in developing the levels of individual competency that are required for championship efforts?

We found the formula for developing excellence in competency to be rather simple, but costly. The five ingredients seem to be:

1. Hard work

2. Focus on the fundamentals

3. Recruiting the most capable people

4. A lifetime of learning

5. Know your limits

Hard Work

Sometimes we forget the truth in some of the most basic value statements we learn as children. If there is anything that we need to be reminded of, it is that nothing worthwhile comes easily. The great teams we observed were made up of individuals who were willing to work hard for countless hours to achieve personal excellence.

As we enjoyed the rehearsal and then the evening performance of the New York Philharmonic Orchestra, we marveled at the competence of every member. Carl Schiebler, director of orchestra personnel, had reminded us earlier in the day that these were probably the most talented musicians in the world. He explained that while many of the orchestra members are gifted musicians, no one has enough natural talent to be selected as a member on the basis of natural ability alone. Even the most gifted must spend tens of thousands of hours developing their ability. At a very early age, when most of their friends were playing games or enjoying the company of other children, these performers began working very hard to develop their gifts and began to pay the price for excellence in individual competence.

It is also important to note that competency is not something that is developed once and for all; it must be maintained. Schiebler told us that in order for the orchestra to achieve peak performance, the musicians must practice individually on a daily basis. An accomplished musician himself, Schiebler says if you miss a day of practice, "you know it. Miss two days and your fellow musicians know it. Miss three days and the audience knows."

At the risk of sounding rather parental, we have observed that today's typical young American worker seems to lack an appreciation for the value of hard work. Certainly there are individual young people who understand what is required to achieve excellence, but as a group, something seems to be lacking. For that matter, it also seems that a large number of older workers have lost their appreciation for hard work.

We had the privilege of watching Jody Conradt lead her team through a practice session in "The Superdrum" on the campus of the University of Texas in Austin. The young women who are members of her team quickly learn the value of hard work. Coach Conradt says that many of the players who become members of her team are gifted athletes who didn't have to work hard to be stars in high school. They quickly learn that to be a member of the Lady Longhorns, Coach Conradt has only one expectation of them: achieve your full potential.

Coach Conradt tells the story of one very talented freshman whose work habits were not fully developed when she arrived at the University of Texas. This young

woman had great difficulty making it through the grueling workouts during the early part of her first season as
a Lady Longhorn. In fact, she didn't make it through any
of the early workouts without collapsing in tears. After
one particularly difficult workout, the young woman appeared in Coach Conradt's office and stated that she
needed to see a doctor. "Something is wrong with me,"
she said. Coach Conradt immediately arranged for the
player to see a physician for a complete examination.

The day after the examination, the young woman
returned to the coach's office with a big smile on her face.
"Did you see the doc," the coach asked? "Yes," was the
simple reply. "Well," Coach Conradt asked rather anx-
iously, "what did he say?" The young woman answered
meekly, "He said that there isn't anything wrong with
me." "Did he say anything else?" Conradt continued. "Well,
yes. I asked him if when it feels like I'm about to die in
practice, am I?" "What did he say?" Coach Conradt asked
seriously. "He said no. Coach, I'm ready to get with it!"

This young woman had actually thought that the
pain that came from pushing herself to the limit was not
normal. Real dream team leaders know that the price of
personal excellence is extremely high in terms of self-
discipline, hard work, and dedication and that pain is
normal!

Focus On The Fundamentals

Coach John Wooden believes excellence in the fundamentals is the key to success in any team effort. In his
"Pyramid of Success," Coach Wooden defines skill as "a
knowledge of and the ability to properly and quickly execute the fundamentals—be prepared and cover every little
detail." As organizations have become increasingly aware
of the intensity of the competition they face, those that
have responded successfully have returned to an empha-

sis on the fundamentals. For a business, that can mean excellent customer service, innovative cost cutting, improved production efficiency, and an uncompromising determination to produce quality goods and services. For a family, such a focus could include spending time together; demonstrations of love, care, and concern; and simply living out the basic values that it espouses. For an educational institution, it may mean that reading, writing, computational, critical thinking, and collaboration skills form the core of all activities.

In the most successful organizations, these fundamentals have been emphasized to the point that the team members perform them without having to consciously think about them; they become instinctive. The members of these great organizations work together instinctively to seize every opportunity to provide, for example, great customer service in the same spirit that one basketball player will, in the wink of an eye, serve up a perfect lob pass to his teammate who will conclude the play with a dramatic slam-dunk for two points!

Within business organizations, families, or athletic teams, this type of spectacular team performance is no random occurrence. It is the result of hours of practice and relentless attention to detail. Coach Wooden's practices *always* devoted significant time to drills that focused on the fundamentals and their associated details.

A story about Paul "Bear" Bryant, the late coach of the University of Alabama's football team, demonstrates his belief in relentless attention to detail. One day during a practice, a visitor observed Coach Bryant doing something that aroused his curiosity. From time to time during the practice, the coach would reach into his pocket, pull out a crumpled little piece of paper, read it, and then put it back in his pocket. The visitor watched him do this several times during the practice and then finally mustered up the courage to ask the coach what was written on the paper. Coach Bryant simply smiled, pulled out the crumpled paper, and let the visitor read it himself. It said, "It's the itty bitty, teeny tiny things that get you beat!"

Indeed, it is the details that can make all the difference. Appropriate focus on the fundamentals can make winning, however winning is defined, more likely and more consistent by minimizing risk and increasing predictability. When we asked Lt. Colonel Steve Trent how he could justify taking the risk inherent in flying F-16s so close together (sometimes eighteen inches apart) at such high speeds (450 m.p.h.), he had a surprising reply: "There is no risk." "Excuse me?" we asked. Trent went on to explain that his team began training for their very complicated show by practicing the most basic flight maneuvers until they achieved perfection. Only then would they begin to add, step by step, the complicated, intricate maneuvers that make their performances so spectacular. In fact, close analysis of the Thunderbirds' shows reveals that the more complex maneuvers are simply the sum of a multitude of very simple, fundamental skills that are performed perfectly. When the time for the first show arrives, so much practice and attention to the basics have taken place that the risk, in what appears to be a very dangerous show, has been minimized.

Recruitment And Selection Of The Most Capable People

Identifying and then recruiting the best people to become team members is one of the most important and obvious activities required if a team is to achieve greatness. However, there are some cases where the selection process does not usually apply. For example, teachers rarely have the opportunity to select the students who are members of their classes. Parents do not have the opportunity to consciously select their children, except in cases of adoption. However, in most situations, teams have the potential to make a significant difference in their probabilities for success by taking a very serious and complete approach to the selection of team members.

Even in the case of American families, the two leaders (supposedly the wife and husband) who create the core of the unit select each other. The thoughtful, rational, reasonable approach to selecting a mate is very familiar to anyone who has ever listened to their parents' advice about dating. Of course, the "love factor" is assumed to be the deciding factor that creates enduring family units willing to make lifetime commitments to one another. Family partnerships require so much of each member that it seems reasonable to predict that love is required for the relationship to thrive.

Lou Whittaker told us that selecting the right team members was the single most important factor in successfully achieving a climbing mission. The selection process he uses helps to assure that a talented, well-balanced team is assembled. The first team member is selected by Whittaker, with a special eye to backup support and leadership skills. Once two of the six to eight individuals have been selected, the two get together and select the third member. They typically ask each other, "Who is the strongest person you can think of, the best climber you have ever climbed with? Who contributed the most to making a tough climb successful?" After the three have been selected, they get together and select the fourth member, beginning to pay particular attention to any special roles on the team that need to be filled. The four members then meet to select the fifth, the five select the sixth, etc., until all of the members have been chosen. As might be expected, agreement on who will become a team member becomes progressively more difficult as the process continues. Getting five people to agree on the sixth member is much more difficult than getting three members to agree on who the fourth member will be. Whittaker noted that because of the increasingly high expectations that come from additional members being involved in the selection process, it is not unusual for the members who are selected last to prove to be the strongest team members.

Lou Whittaker said he looks for a wide range of qualities in the mountaineers who constitute his climbing teams. These qualities range from technical climbing skills to team-oriented attitudes to basic hygiene practices.

> When we were on Everest there were times when the storms were so bad that we couldn't leave the tent for five to seven days. Can you imagine sharing a two-person tent with someone who doesn't brush his teeth for seven days? We actually talk about these types of things when we are selecting people—you can't get too basic.

We asked Lou Whittaker to put aside all modesty and tell us why he is considered by the climbing community to be the greatest climber/leader. We asked him what his greatest personal accomplishment is. His answer was clear and direct: "Staying alive!" He had already told us that almost all of his peers in his age group (late fifties) who had been active climbers for thirty years or more had lost their lives in climbing accidents. We asked him to account for his survival when the probabilities certainly were not in his favor. "Through a lot of luck and a little skill," he modestly responded. Some other mountaineers we talked with said his survival could more realistically be attributed to significant luck, a tremendous amount of skill, and extremely good judgment. Whittaker, who was fifty-four at the time of our interview, said:

> There's old climbers, and there's bold climbers, but there are no old, bold climbers. This means that you've finally got conservative enough to climb safely. Some

of the stuff you did as a youngster, you wonder how in the world you got away with it. I'm not hesitant at all to tell people I'm teaching about the accidents I've been in and the mistakes I've made and the number of people I've carried out that have made mistakes.

Whittaker pointed out that while the motivation for his willingness to go on many rescues has clearly been his concern for his fellow climbers, he has not missed an opportunity to learn from the mistakes this tragic activity has revealed. Gaining wisdom and judgment from the experience of others, especially their mistakes, can speed the development of competency and make it much less painful. Whittaker always looks for opportunities to improve his climbing and leadership skills by learning everything he can from the other team members. The value of outstanding teammates becomes pretty obvious when we realize that these are the people from whom we learn the most. Whittaker put it this way:

> I've always thought that when you guide, you only become as good as the people you guide. That would also be true for a leader, I guess. When you lead, you're only as good as the people you lead. I have drawn talents from a lot of different individuals that I've taken up mountains...such as Robert McNamara, Dick Bass [the first man to climb the seven continents of the world], Frank Wells [president of Warner Brothers at the time], and numerous others.

General Brady said:

> You've got to have faith in the crew-chief who maintains the aircraft and in the guy next to you, your co-pilot. And that's a result of their training and your training. They must continually strive to improve their skills—they can never rest on where they are. Never, never stop working on your skills!

Know Your Limits

These examples serve to demonstrate that there are at least two major dimensions to the concept of trust. One is very closely related to the team practice of mutual support and trust. This dimension addresses the question, "Can I count on you to be there when I need you?" It is very much a question of an "other-oriented" attitude which says that you value me to the degree you are willing to risk part of yourself with me. The second dimension of trust is directly related to the concept of individual competence. The question now becomes not just are you *willing* to support me, but do you have the *ability* (competency) to support me. An attitude of support is of little practical value to a team unless the team members possess the knowledge, skill, and ability to put this attitude into action.

When Lou Whittaker's mountain climbing teams encountered danger in the form of ice and snow, strong winds, or the steepness of the slope, their response was to tie themselves together with climbing ropes. In so doing, they committed themselves to support the safety of their teammates, even to the point of risking their own lives in an attempt to save others. If a person lower down the mountain than you falls, the risk of them causing you to fall is not as great because they would not have time to gather too much momentum before the slack in the line is gone. However, if a teammate at a higher elevation falls, the risk to the supporter is much greater because it is more difficult to break their fall. Whittaker says that it's a sobering process to decide "whose rope I am willing to hook into. They not only must have the willingness to support and take a risk for me—they must also have the skill and ability to support me. They must know what they're doing!"

When we interviewed Whittaker at the base of Mt. Rainier, he invited us to come back some time and climb

Rainier with the help of his guides at Rainier Mountain-eering. When Bob, his daughter Kelly, and his son Rob took Lou up on his offer, they learned what he was talking about experientially. The 14,000+-foot summit of Rainier is very nearly the highest in the continental United States. The summit climb, which begins at about 5000 feet and is largely over snow, ice, and glaciers (all year), is considered by most serious climbers to be the most difficult endurance climb in the lower forty-eight states.

The climb began for Bob, Kelly, and Rob at 9:00 on a Saturday morning and ended thirty-two hours later at 5 p.m. on Sunday, with only five hours of rest at Camp Muir on the way up the mountain. The wind blew relentlessly at thirty to forty miles an hour and the temperature at the summit was eighteen degrees. Needless to say, this was no "walk in the park," but the Fisher team had trained long and hard for this opportunity and felt confident as the climb proceeded.

After the five-hour rest at Camp Muir, the trek resumed at midnight. (It is important to get past certain points before the sun rises and begins to melt the ice. Besides, it takes that long to get up and down while spending only one night on the mountain.) Soon after sunrise, the climbing team took a very brief ten-minute rest stop at a point appropriately named "Disappointment Cleaver." This rock out-cropping is at the top of a particularly steep section of the climb. Bob welcomed the rest stop more than anyone could imagine. While he was really hurting, he remained confident and determined that he could make it to the summit, now just two to three hours away.

His first clue of trouble came when he realized he was having trouble chewing a Snickers candy bar and then swallowing. When the tough, demanding, and by now hated guide Leslie bounced by, she asked him, "How ya doing, Bob?" His slurred reply told the whole story: "I'm dooing ook—I'm gooing tooo the toop!" Suddenly

Leslie's face showed the first sign of concern and kindness that Bob had seen over the entire trip. "You don't sound okay, Bob. I think you're out of O [oxygen]. You better go down." Bob argued determinedly (and pitifully), "I'll beee ook, I'm gooing tooo the top!" Leslie's reply provides a classic team lesson:

> I don't think you're okay, Bob. You have altitude sickness and you need to go down. I'm going to give you a few minutes to decide what to do, but do two things for me. Look in front of you to see who's hooked into your rope. Then look behind you to see who's hooked into your rope. Do you want to take the chance that you might slip and fall and endanger their lives just because you think you want to make the summit?

What a tough question. Bob looked at Kelly, who was hooked into the rope ahead of him, and Rob, who was right behind. The answer to this tough question was easy. When Leslie returned in a few minutes, Bob unhooked from the rope and pointed down the mountain.

Whose rope are you willing to hook into? Leaders need to consider how this question applies to each member of the team. If there is a member who you would not be willing to trust, ask yourself why not. If the answer is that they lack the skill, ability, or knowledge, then it becomes the leader's responsibility to coach, teach, and train.

"JUST GETTING TOGETHER AND TALKING"

PRACTICE #6: EMPOWERING COMMUNICATION

Team Taurus was the first massive process we went through where we started with the team idea almost at the beginning. We brought people into the team from all the different areas of the company where always before by and large we'd done things sequentially...

Communication before was what our people here at the company started to call our chimney problem, where all the different functions acted as if they were within their own isolated chimney and they couldn't break out of their chimney to talk to somebody in another chimney. All they could do was send their ideas up to the top, and by the time you went through several layers, you got to the top person in manufacturing. Another chimney was working to the top of engineering. The positions were so hardened that when the people that technically were now going to compromise tried to do it, it was just hardly possible.

But in Team Taurus we were unofficially breaking out of the chimney early and problems that we would have had the old way were solved in a very unofficial, informal way—nothing written, just getting together and talking about the best ways to do things.

Don Petersen

The issue of "chimney communication" versus "just getting together and talking about the best ways to do things" is relevant to many teams. Don Petersen's group grappled with the issue of a cumbersome and sluggish organizational structure and communication process that simply were not working. They learned a much better way from their own internal Taurus project.

From huge teams to small teams, from manufacturing to service, from business to volunteer groups, we found lack of shared information and easy access to relevant information to be the number one roadblock to effective teamwork. In many cases, as with Ford, the "chimney problem" was the internal system for communication which had to change. It was particularly difficult to communicate and get the necessary information quickly from people outside the immediate team.

How was Team Taurus different? In order to get total involvement, quick information, and make the best decisions, all the key team players were a part of the team project from the beginning, including the customers. The question posed to dealers and salespeople, as well as engineers, manufacturing people, designers, and marketers was, "Tell us what you think." And all of these people could talk to each other without getting someone else's permission. This certainly makes sense. When the mindset is team and when the time frame is urgent, it makes sense that we talk to each other—*now*. We share information and we ask for feedback because it is the only way we know for teammates and teams to obtain accurate data and make informed decisions.

Picture this scene. You've probably seen it over and over. The pass play wasn't successful, and the quarterback and receiver walk back to the huddle or off the field together. They are talking. And if they are winners, they are talking about what they need to do differently next time. They are not wasting energy blaming each other. They are giving information and getting feedback—immediately—sharing and getting, and increasing the odds that the play will be successful next time. This is empowered communication.

Translate the above scenario to your team environment. What are the barriers that keep people from talking directly to each other? What feedback does your team need to get from another team or from the people you serve? How can you run better plays, improve your service, foster relationships, enhance your quality, or develop ownership of your mission without empowered communication?

Empowerment

What a potent concept! Empowerment is creating the conditions that facilitate the best efforts of people, by removing the barriers that inhibit the use of individual talent, creativity, and energy. Empowerment gives people permission to utilize their full potential. Leaders of work teams, volunteer teams, church teams, and family teams must indeed "give permission" to team members to think, be innovative, get involved, and take risks. Without leader permission and acceptance, or empowerment, people assume it is best to protect themselves by holding back, giving safe responses, and making tentative commitments.

We deliberately chose to examine the "group life" of real dream teams that simply could not have reached their compelling missions without extraordinary effort. Without exception, the teams represented by our team leaders consciously realized the need to create an atmosphere and a system that rewarded open communication. Poor communication could cost lives in Steve Trent's Thunderbird flying team, in Lou Whittaker's climbing team, or in General Brady's rescue team. In Don Petersen and Don Tyson's teams, poor communication meant slower responses to customer needs. In all cases, empowering communication increased the odds for best-effort responses.

Another way of viewing empowerment, and one that is an overriding principle for front-line supervisors, is visualizing all actions as either enhancing or damaging self-esteem. The norm is to engage in interactions with others in ways that enhance or maintain self-esteem. When teams accept this norm, talk about it, and intentionally put it into practice, it directly affects the way people communicate with each other. People focus on things that need to be done and behaviors that need to be changed. The focus is not on putting people down, blaming others, personalizing, or damaging self-esteem.

A vice-president in a mid-sized southwestern insurance company recently described the very painful process of downsizing his staff as a result of business conditions. He recounted a very sensitive and respectful approach to talented individuals who were experiencing a sudden and unwanted termination. Every effort had been made to maintain self-esteem in a most difficult situation. Even in the toughest of times, respect and esteem can be honored.

People work best in environments that facilitate best efforts and remove inhibiting barriers. They need permission through clearly communicated norms regarding teamwork and risk taking simply because most people assume a defensive posture due to previous negative work experiences.

Finally, your own experience regarding your own best efforts should immediately validate the necessary conditions for empowerment. All people work best in environments that enhance and build self-esteem.

The most critical element of empowerment is communication—what and how the leader communicates and the norms or standards for communication within the team. As with the other six practices we found in great teams, what is communicated and how it is communicated must be thoughtful, deliberate, and intentionally designed to convey messages and signals that encourage people to give their best effort, work with others, and direct activities toward the common mission.

The consequence of a communication failure could be of major proportions. Arthur Schlesinger, Jr., for example, when reflecting on the communication process in President Kennedy's cabinet prior to the ill-fated Bay of Pigs decision, lamented the fact that he withheld some of his personal reservations about the plan because it seemed that everyone else felt confident. He didn't want to disrupt the cohesiveness and apparent consensus. Schlesinger's assumption was flawed on two counts. First, others really did have doubts and, second, in decision making, even one team member's reservation can be the catalyst for a better decision. The groupthink phenomenon can only be overcome with open, honest communication.

The Abilene paradox is a story popularized by Jerry Harvey. In this true boyhood story, he tells of a hot and sweaty summer afternoon when he and his family decided to drive fifty-three miles to Abilene, which nobody really wanted to do, in an unairconditioned family car, which nobody really wanted to ride in, to eat dinner at a place where nobody really wanted to eat! How did this very common communication glitch occur? Each person thought every other person wanted to go, and for the sake of harmony, no one expressed disagreement. It was as simple and as absurd as that.

Real dream teams devote time and energy to building and rewarding communication networks that keep people "from going to Abilene." Miscommunications that cause us to end up in Abilene waste time, energy, and money and make a lot of people unhappy. Flexible, innovative, quick-response teams can't afford such waste. As the previous examples suggest, managing agreement can be just as tough as managing conflict. Today's teams must do both.

Practicing Empowering Communication

The goal of empowered communication is to share information openly and helpfully. But what information is appropriate to share? The answer is any information that will help any person or team do a better job. Who knows what information is needed? The person doing the job and the team doing the work know. Nobody knows the job better than the one who does it every day. Team leaders, then, are facilitators. They help teams and team members get the information they need to do their jobs, or play their roles.

People search for answers to three critical communication questions before they commit to working in any open team environment:

- Are you willing to listen to me?

- Are you willing to share the information I need to help me do my job well?

- Are you willing to include me in decisions that affect me?

A very useful communication model for creating greater self-awareness and motivation to change was introduced by Joseph Luft and Harry Ingram (see next page). The model helps people easily visualize the dynamic interactive nature of the communication process. In addition, assessment tools are available to help team members assess their degree of willingness to listen and share information in an interdependent team environment.

Johari Window Model

	Information Known to You	Information Unknown to You
Information Known to Team	Open Arena (You and team share)	Blind Spot (Team knows— you don't)
Information Unknown to Team	Facade (You know— team does not)	Unutilized Potential (Nobody knows)

Increased Ability to Seek Feedback

0   100%

Increased Ability to Share Information	Open Arena	Blind Spot
	* Solve Problems Due to Feedback and Shared Information	* Problems Occur Due to Poor Feedback
	• Increase Open Arena Increase Teamwork	* Increase Feedback, Reduce Blind Spots
	Facade	Underutilized Potential
	* Problems Occur Due to Lack of Information	* Problems Occur Due to Lack of Awareness
	* Increase Shared Information, Reduce Facades	* Increase Feedback and Shared Information, Reduce Underutilized Potential

100%

Measuring and assessing at designated intervals is a critical component of quality teamwork. Since open communication is a desired norm in the new team environment, teams can increase their team arena by seeking feedback regularly and sharing results with each other.

We ask the three basic questions (Will you listen to me? Are you willing to share information? Are you willing to include me in decisions that affect me?) in the context of the Johari Window model.

In a team environment, the communication goal and communication standards center around increasing the team's ability to open the "shared information" or "open arena" window as widely as possible. While the window does not have to stay open all the time, the ability of a team and team members to open the window to access relevant data at a moment's notice is a critical issue. Teams that do not have the ability to open that window quickly smother from the toxic fumes of slow response, poor service, and mediocrity in the fulfillment of their mission.

Are You Willing To Listen To Me?

It was Sunday, April 14, 1912. By 10 p.m., at least seven wireless warnings about ice had reached the ship. Although officers anticipated reaching the ice field by 9:30 p.m., the ship pushed on through the night at 22 knots, at unslackened speed. The last warning came about 11 p.m. from the ship California, less than ten miles away. "Say, old man, we are stuck here, surrounded by ice." From the Titanic came these words, "Shut up, shut up. Keep out. I am talking to Cape Race. You are jamming my signals." At 11:40 p.m., the inevitable happened. An iceberg was hit. Two and one-half hours later, the Titanic sank. Hundreds perished.

In order to avoid daily "Titanic" results, team members and teams must not only be willing to receive feedback from others when offered, they must also actively solicit feedback from those with whom they work or serve. How I am doing? How does my work affect you? What do you need from my team that will help your team when they come on duty? These questions solicit feedback. In a team environment, people do better work when others feed back to them helpful information regarding their work. People need both positive feedback and corrective feedback. Effective teamwork through empowering communication calls for active listening and the ability to seek out feedback. Donald Petersen from Ford told us:

> We soon found that there had to be a receptive ear embedded in the superstructure of supervision and management. Participative management had to be a corollary to employee involvement or there is no place for employee ideas to go.

All people like to be heard. Listening conveys value to what is being said and to the person sharing the information. Psychologically, it is one of the most powerful vehicles for confirming the importance of another human being. To listen is to provide undivided attention long enough to confirm what we have heard the other person say. Most of us can count on the fingers of one hand the people who truly listen consistently when we speak.

Yet listening is the most underused people skill. Whether in family teams or organizational teams, the story is the same. We spend little time truly listening with total focus on the other person's agenda. The communication norm, unfortunately, is the listener tuned in to his or her personal agenda, selectively hearing what he or she wants to hear and looking for information to support his or her own thinking process. Would you believe that some parents, for example, spend less than two minutes a day with an individual child giving undivided attention to the child's agenda? Most team leaders, when they do analyze how they spend their time, are amazed at how little time they spend deliberately, naively listening for the sole purpose of getting feedback or information from members of their team.

Toyota listens. As a result, each week Toyota implements thousands of suggestions from people at all levels. Marriott wants you to remember their service and encourages you to share your feedback in writing either during or after your stay. Cadillac follows up your service visit with a phone call. A winner of the coveted Malcolm Baldrige Award, Cadillac has proven that listening to customers and servicing their needs is a win–win deal. The bottom line is that the only way we can accurately know what others think or feel is to ask, listen, and demonstrate that we value what we hear. Lou Whittaker believes in listening:

> It is important to listen, even when you feel certain you are correct. One time, we wasted eight days waiting for the snows to settle, but I had been in a few avalanches so I had more experience than those who hadn't been in avalanches. I dug a lot of people out, so I could say, "This is a slope that we could lose our whole party on. I think we should turn around." But instead of saying "we should turn around," I say, "I think we should turn around" and then we talk it over. That's an example of trying to get the best out of everybody. We can get the best of everybody only when we keep valuing those around us, making sure that we don't have blind spots.

Great teams are teams that fully utilize the talents of all the team members. These teams capitalize on the unique roles that people play and take advantage of individual differences. In the earlier discussion of the team practice of clear roles, we emphasized the direct motivational link between individual roles and the overall mission of the team. If I believe I count, I make a difference.

If the team needs me, I will do my best. Real dream teams activate the importance of each role through listening, valuing ideas, and prizing individual differences and unique contributions.

Do we listen to each other? Am I heard around here? Do others value my ideas? People don't take long to answer these questions. If your answer to these questions is no in terms of your work team, it wouldn't be surprising to find that you and others are not committed to giving best effort. Why should you? Why should they?

Good teams need ways to get regular feedback from people on the team, other teams with whom they work, and people they serve. The key is not waiting until others initiate the feedback. The key is to go and get it!

"The leader better be listening or he's dead," says rescue helicopter pilot General Brady. "People have to be able to give you feedback at any moment. If somebody sees something on the instrument panel that I'd overlooked or if I had been blinded by a flare or something, or don't see an obstacle of some kind, it is understood that they say, 'Stop!'" That is why the team is so important.

One operator's machine consistently required repair, resulting in costly down time. A new supervisor asked the operator what he thought the problem was and what he thought could be done to fix the machine. The supervisor used a prodding process to get the machine operator to take his question seriously. The supervisor listened and then convinced the repair personnel to try out the operator's suggestion. His suggestion worked and saved the company several thousand dollars. The supervisor went back and asked the operator how long he had the idea about what it would take to keep his machine running. Seems he had the solution for over a year. The supervisor asked why he hadn't shared it. "Nobody ever asked!" was the reply. And that is what happens when the environment does not support regular listening and feedback.

How good are you at getting out and soliciting the ideas of those around you? Do you have a regular plan for listening to your teammates, customers, or family members? ("Regular" and "plan" are the key words here.) Do you know which members of your team, family, or staff feel more comfortable sharing ideas on an individual, one-on-one basis or in a group setting? Do you ask for feedback verbally as well as in written form?

When people give you feedback or share ideas with you, do you let them know that you appreciate their input? If you use someone's idea, do you credit that person for the idea? If you don't use suggestions, do you convey appreciation for the input anyway?

Think of the reactions you value most from others when you share ideas or make suggestions.

Listening is the communication tool to remove blind spots. The Johari Window demonstrates that when you increase your ability to seek out feedback and get more information, you are likely to confirm some things you suspected while discovering some surprises and uncovering some blind spots. Blind spots are simply capsules of information of which others are aware and you are not. Have you ever seen a videotape of yourself in action or recorded yourself making a presentation? Did you see or hear anything that surprised you? You bet you did—little speech patterns, mannerisms, accents, or habits you didn't know you had. Every person has them. Every department in every company has them. We only discover blind spots when we pay attention.

Got any blind spots? LISTEN. Then, ACT!

Are You Willing To Share Information?

Team leaders and team members must view information as power they want to share with each other as opposed to power to be hoarded or protected. It is not unusual for traditional managers to deliberately withhold information they believe others do not need or to use information as leverage for things they want. It is important to emphasize that holding out relevant data from others in a team environment damages credibility and kills trust.

"Most catastrophes on the battlefield or anyplace or anywhere are the result of the lack of communication. Poor communication leads to catastrophic results," says General Brady. How much information do people need? Let them tell you. Enough to do their job well. Enough to make informed decisions. Enough to empower them to solve problems and take action quickly.

"The dilemma," suggests Ford's Petersen, "is how to get enough power or enough authority to the team from the organization superstructure. You simply must give the team the power to be able to make on-the-spot judgments, decisions, so the team can move on to the next issue. We've got to get the superstructure leaders accepting the idea that they must empower the team."

One of the most effective tools for discovering information that needs to be shared is to ask. Ask others around you what information you have that they need. It's as simple as that. Some will say they want clearer expectations from you regarding job performance. Some will say they want you to share more information with them prior to making a decision that affects them. Others will indicate they want more feedback from you, both positive and critical, regarding their contribution to the team.

Note that it is a strength of team leadership, whether you are a product manager or a parent, to open yourself up to feedback. Here, the issue is how to communicate or share information in more helpful ways. Regardless of the team skill you want to improve, do not view the suggestions you get as bad news or indicative of weakness on your part. Remember that it is good news to get information about a roadblock to team effectiveness, even if you are contributing to the roadblock. You cannot fix it if you do not know about it. Ignorance is not bliss.

The bottom line is that if you ask the people around you what information they need from you, be sure to listen to what they say. Soak it up. Clarify. Understand. Learn. Traditional managers often kill the messenger. Great team leaders learn. And in the process, they get more and better information. They learn how they can empower others.

The information gained from listening tells you what you need to share, but knowing what you need to share is only half the battle. The other half is sharing the needed information in a form in which it can be used. MIS (management information systems) departments are legendary for generating huge quantities of unusable data. They disperse the information in a form that makes sense to other MIS people, period. Having the information is only part of the solution. Translating the information you have in ways that are meaningful to your team completes the communication loop.

Based on Ford Motor Company's experience prior to Team Taurus, the whole system for sharing information had to change. Tyson Foods increased its information flow to people on the production line by giving them more information about the Tyson mission and how they made a difference by reaching clear daily standards in production and quality. Tyson Foods deliberately trained managers and their supervisors to work together to solve common team problems.

Note Sybil Mobley's comments about shared information: "The team concept is crucial in business. You just aren't going to make it unless you operate as a team. You know, can you work with others? I have an executive committee and all I can do is take a proposal. And it never leaves there like it went in. And that's when I begin to feel we are hitting the mark. And at first they felt obligated to agree and then they realized that wasn't the point. And it is just amazing what brainstorming and sharing and feeding on each other's ideas can do."

It is amazing what sharing information can do. Part of the magic in teamwork comes from shared information. It removes blind spots and erodes facades. In short, it enlarges the arena of shared information and thus empowers communicators and the communication process.

As John Wooden so aptly put it, "The leader must be interested in finding the best way, not in having his own way."

Are You Willing To Include Me In Decisions That Affect Me?

A third question must be answered affirmatively if one commits to giving his or her best effort in a team environment: "Are you willing to include me in decisions that affect me?" The traditional manager sarcastically says, "Big deal." Team leaders in the new environment who want the best from everybody enthusiastically say, "Big deal!" The big deal is that people are much more likely to implement and have ownership of those decisions in which they have been included. Ownership is the essence of teaming. If I have a part in the planning, I will be more likely to implement the plan. It is also true that people resist those decisions that are forced upon them from outside or from above. If others must implement a plan, the rule of thumb is to include them in the planning.

Is more up-front time needed when including in the decision-making process those who later must implement the decision? Yes. Is there less resistance, fewer false starts, less rework, and less dissatisfaction? Yes. Is there increased innovation, more efficiency over the long term, better decisions, higher participation, and more "best effort?" Again, yes.

Do the communication process and communication system allow open, shared communication? Is information easily accessed? Is the information presented in forms that are easily understood by users? Do people on your team communicate in ways that build self-esteem? These are critical indicators of empowering communication. And these basic questions can be easily answered by any team leader who wants to be stronger through increased feedback, reduced facades, and, as Sybil Mobley put it, "brainstorming and sharing and feeding on each other's ideas."

"Show-Time"

Five F-16 jets are in a tight formation as they begin one of their many difficult aerial maneuvers at speeds approaching 500 m.p.h. Excellence and survival depend on listening and sharing information and clearly understanding the procedure. There is no room for miscommunication. Time and time again during "show-time" for the Thunderbirds, the arena of shared information is wide open. Listening and sharing, listening and sharing—no maneuver is begun until every piece of information is checked off and verified.

Every team can identify "show-time" moments when accurate information and communication are essential. It may be a procedure for a shift change for nursing teams, a procedure to confirm pledges for a United Way team, or a procedure to verify daily assignments for a city street repair team. "Show-time" moments are those times when easy communication and shared information result in wins or miscommunication results in losses.

To build the size of the open arena area in team communication, consider the following:

1. Identify "show-time" moments in communication, those times when the team needs to nail down a standard procedure for communicating.

2. Identify what information needs to be shared.

3. Identify how the information will be shared.

4. Identify how the information will be received or confirmed.

5. Have a procedure for correcting communication glitches.

In Team Taurus, blind spots and facades were removed by eliminating the "chimney" system. The basic motivation for improving systems for better feedback and more shared, relevant information is the awareness that the present communication system is not working. "Linear information, linear thinking, and incremental strategies are no match for the turbulence of today's business climate," assert Bennis and Nanus in *Leaders*. No one has to blame anybody. The motivation for change comes from poor results.

Post Cereals, Jonesboro, Arkansas

In this new location of Post Cereals, self-managing teams got the nod as the strategy of choice, the process on which all operations would be based. The leadership team members were selected because of their commitment to innovative, participatory concepts. They wanted to be a part of a process that would make a difference. The selection process was based on proven technical competency and a willingness to work in a team environment.

Here's how they operationalized their commitment to teamwork through creating a system to enlarge and sustain an arena of open communication:

1. The seven practices of highly effective teams became central to their teamwork approach.

2. They committed to teamwork in their statement of mission.

3. Communication and open dialogue were identified as one of their five core values.

4. The signatures of the team members appear on the huge mission statement that greets people at the facility entrance.

5. They adopted a Star Management system to foster maximum participation and cross-functional diversity.

6. All members of the start-up team assessed their social interaction style. They also assessed and measured their ability to seek feedback from teammates as well as their ability to freely share information with teammates. Johari Window profiles resulted.

7. Based on their increased understanding of the social interaction and communication styles of self and others, team members actively negotiated with each other regarding how best to talk to each other to assure open communication and easy access to information.

8. One-on-one discussions took place between all team members who identified work dependencies on each other. Written "deals" were made to help guide healthy daily interactions and problem solving.

9. Teams have quick access to meetings or "team huddle" rooms.

10. Regular educational opportunities are created to identify communication roadblocks and teach productive strategies for overcoming them.

"RESPECT WITHOUT FEAR"

PRACTICE #7:
WINNING ATTITUDE

"That's okay—we'll come back." That was the message a national television audience could have overheard by reading the lips of Notre Dame head football coach Lou Holtz as his defensive team came to the sidelines. The Miami Hurricanes had just scored the go-ahead touchdown late in their 1990 game against Holtz's Fighting Irish. To the casual observer, it didn't seem all that certain that Notre Dame would come back. They were playing a truly outstanding opponent that seemed to be taking charge of the game. However, as they so often do, the Fighting Irish did come back and did win the game.

Why is it that some teams and organizations seem to win more often than would be expected given the level of their talent and their circumstances? Part of the answer surely lies in the sense of motivation that comes from dedication to a clear mission. However, a positive, winning attitude that expects success provides the "magic" that brings a team or group more than its share of victories.

Attitude Is Everything

When we asked Lou Holtz to identify the most important ingredient in building championship teams, he focused on attitude:

> Real simple—one's attitude. Attitude is where it all starts. It's your choice, the type of attitude you have. Attitude towards yourself, towards other people, towards challenges—just attitude. I want the right attitude and I won't compromise on it. Some things you might compromise on; I won't compromise on attitude. You have attitude, you have teamwork. If you have teamwork, you have a good product. If you have a good product, you have success. It all starts with attitude.

It is important to provide a working definition of the concept of attitude. An attitude is a predisposition to respond to situations in a certain manner. A winning attitude then means that a person is predisposed to respond to a challenge with the positive expectation that the challenge will be met.

Wherever he goes, Lou Holtz seems to build a winning attitude into his team effort. When he was the coach of the Arkansas Razorbacks in 1978, he led his team to a very successful season that culminated in an Orange Bowl match-up with the University of Oklahoma Sooners. The Sooners were huge favorites from the beginning, but when Coach Holtz suspended three star players for rule violations just a few days before the game, the Las Vegas bookmakers removed the match from the betting board.

Holtz noticed during practices that the attitudes of his players became increasingly negative as the game approached. But by the time the game arrived, one newscaster reported that he had never seen a team charge out of the dressing room and onto the field with such passion and excitement as the Arkansas Razorbacks did that day.

Later, when he asked Holtz what he had said to get his team so charged up, Holtz replied, "I told them that Oklahoma is the biggest, meanest, and toughest team I've ever coached against—and the last eleven players out of this dressing room are going to have to start!"

Anyone who knows Lou Holtz knows that he is famous for his clever wit. They also know he is fiercely competitive. You can bet the preceding quote is an example of his after-the-fact wit and not something that actually happened. According to Jim Elliot, who was one of the players on that team, Coach Holtz had dealt with the team's attitude just a couple of days before the game. After noticing much negative thinking on the part of his players, Holtz called a team meeting. He called the meeting to order, approached the large chalkboard in the room, and said, "I'm tired of all of the talk about how we don't have a chance to win this game. We're not leaving this room until we fill up this chalkboard with reasons why we can win this game." After a period of silence, one player spoke up with a semi-positive statement: "Well, Coach, we've got the best defense in the country against the run, and Oklahoma is a running team—so if they do beat us, it won't be too bad." Holtz wrote the comment on the board, and others began to speak up with increasingly positive statements. Soon the board was full and the room was filled with an entirely different attitude. Jim Elliot says that he left the meeting convinced that Arkansas would win the game, and win it they did by dominating Oklahoma by a score of 33-6.

Great teams expect to win. While they are realistic enough to know that no team wins all of the time, they never enter the competition expecting to lose. And they never get accustomed to losing. They may demonstrate good sportsmanship when they lose, but they *hate losing*. Show us a team that doesn't mind losing and we'll show you a loser! A significant part of many people's motivation to win is rooted in a very sincere fear of failure.

As paradoxical as it may be, defeat does seem to play a role in achieving greatness. The determination and commitment necessary for a championship effort are born out of the ashes of defeat.

From 1982-83 through 1984-85, the University of Texas Lady Longhorns compiled a record of ninety wins and only nine losses. For each of those three seasons, they were generally considered to be the best women's basketball team in the nation. However, they did not make it to the "Final Four" of the NCAA National Championship in any of those three years. Devastating injuries and untimely losses caused the six seniors-to-be to end the 1984-85 season with a sense of frustration, disappointment, and almost bitterness not normally associated with a team that had won over 90 percent of its games.

As Jody Conradt described the 1985-86 Lady Longhorn championship team, she was quick to point out that the seeds for that success were planted in the previous three years, when the team had great success throughout the year only to be deeply disappointed in the national championship tournament.

> [The key to our success was] not in the championship year, but the two prior years. We got down to eight players and went through the conference schedule undefeated and then lost in the regional finals to Louisiana Tech, who's always a power. But that team was incredibly gutsy and close and all of those things that happened to them I think brought them to that point. And not only that year and having to fight back from injury after injury, but the next year we were going to host the Final Four and everybody said, "This is Texas' year and they're going to win it." There was so much pressure on that team—you couldn't believe it. We go off to play in the regionals and everybody's already bought their tickets for the Final Four and they are saying, "Texas is going to get to play on their home court," and we go and lose on a last second shot to Western Kentucky. And it was with one sec-

ond on the game clock. They in-bound the ball and
score. And it goes through and we lose 92-90. That
was the most incredibly difficult thing. I remember
how I felt personally when I got back from that trip
and we had thousands of fans waiting for us at the
airport who were very supportive, and you know that
was awful. You can disappoint yourself and live with
that easier than you live with disappointing a lot of
people. But from that point on, that team just—at
that point they would have steam-rolled anyone in
their path that next year. They came back with that
kind of determination.

I think it was by far the best team I've had—not
necessarily just looking at players talent for talent for
talent, but the fact that they were so cohesive and the
fact that there was such closeness in that group. The
team didn't talk about their disappointment because
it hurt too bad. But you could see them really depend
on each other because you knew that nobody really
understood how you felt except your teammates. There
was a real feeling, "I need you or else I'm not going
to be able to make it through this." What, in my
opinion, brought it all about was the whole sequence
of events that happened for three years before they
got to the championship season. And the more I've
observed and been involved, I believe there almost
has to be some kind of adversity that pulls a team
together.

When the Lady Longhorns' 1984-85 season ended
with a two-point loss (on a "prayer shot" at the buzzer) to
Western Kentucky in the Midwest Regionals, these young
women were faced with a "moment of truth." Coach Jody
Conradt says the Western Kentucky loss hurt more than
any other she has experienced. It hurt the team members, too. Six months later, as the 1985-86 season began,
Kamie Ethridge, the team captain, appeared in Coach
Conradt's office. The coach says Kamie is one of the fierc-
est competitors she has ever coached. She rarely revealed
any "soft" emotions or feelings. So what she said on this

day was a little surprising. Kamie began with a question: "Coach, do you remember that game we lost?" Coach Conradt assured her she did remember. "Well," Kamie continued, "I know how bad that loss hurt you. But I want you to know that it hurt me second worst!"

Coach Conradt works her teams so hard in practice that it is not unusual for players to complain about being tired or hurting. But this team was different. She said that she can't remember one complaint from any of her players during the entire season. When we asked her what she attributed this lack of complaints to, she provided some remarkable insight:

> I think that this team didn't complain about being tired and hurting because they knew what real pain was. Real pain comes from not achieving your potential—from knowing that you're the best but not being able to prove it. The pain that these girls felt in practice and games was minor compared to the pain of the previous two seasons.

Overcoming Adversity

The phenomenon seems to be real. When a team faces severe adversity, one of two outcomes seems to occur. Either a sense of closeness, determination, and commitment emerges from the experience or the team's spirit is broken and the team gives up. We've all experienced this in family, work, and countless other situations. A winning attitude is one that faces adversity as a temporary and occasional occurrence that will not last. To paraphrase Robert Schuller, "Tough times never last, tough people [teams] do!"

A winning attitude can even be detected in the language of people. In our discussions, the great team leaders rejected the use of words like defeat and failure. It wasn't that things always went their way; it was just that they refused to characterize their efforts with negative words that imply a final outcome that is unacceptable. Instead of defeat or failure, they encountered setbacks, delays, obstacles, disappointments, tough lessons, and difficult opportunities. All of these words imply less than full success, but they also communicate a temporary state which they fully expect to improve.

Beginning the evening before a performance, Lt. Colonel Steve Trent and his Thunderbird flight team observe a "blackout period" or quiet time when they rest and avoid interaction with people outside their team. The purpose of this practice is for the team members to prepare themselves, both physically and mentally, for their very demanding performance. The mental aspect of this preparation involves the process of imagining a successful performance. Imagining is pretty much the ultimate in terms of a winning attitude. It involves creating a picture in your mind of the most positive outcome you can imagine. In the case of the Thunderbirds, this involves a "mental video" of a perfect performance of the intricate steps involved in their show. Numerous athletes have reported that this process of mental rehearsal or practice has significantly enhanced their performance.

Thoughts That Kill

We interviewed Lt. Colonel Trent just prior to the beginning of a "blackout period" for the Thunderbirds. As we discussed the work of the Thunderbirds, Trent consistently minimized the degree of risk involved. He pointed out that they had trained so long and so hard on the fundamentals that what appeared to be a dangerous activity was really very safe. We were not convinced and we continued to probe, asking Trent how he could justify risking lives for the sake of entertainment. Showing signs of minor irritation, Lt. Colonel Trent finally said, "There really is no risk." At this point we interjected, "Excuse me, but if there is no risk, what about the 1984 accident?" The reference was to a tragic accident that resulted in the deaths of the entire Thunderbird flight team. The Thunderbirds are trained to take their cues from the commander/leader and to rely on his judgment with their lives. In this heartbreaking accident, an equipment failure in the aircraft of the commander/leader prevented him from successfully completing a maneuver that called for the team to pull out of a dive at the last second. As a result of his equipment failure, all three planes in the diamond formation followed him into the sands of the desert where they were practicing. Our reference to this sad event brought a clear and decisive response from Trent. "Do we have to talk about that? Because if we do, this interview needs to be over!"

Needless to say, we immediately recognized our mistake in pressing this point and told Trent that of course we did not have to talk about this incident. He went on to explain that while he was fully aware of the event, he refused to let himself think such negative thoughts, especially just prior to a performance that required total self-confidence for success. As he spoke, we began to understand why he was somewhat angry with us. We had introduced negative thoughts that had the potential to endanger the lives of Trent and his teammates. "We're not afraid," he went on to say. "We just can't think about negative outcomes—we have to have positive thoughts if we are going to be successful."

Lt. Colonel Trent is an outstanding example of a leader who practices disciplined positive thinking. Surely there are risks and the potential for negative outcomes is genuine in what he does, and Trent knows it. However, he disciplines himself to dwell and meditate on the good, the positive, and success.

The opposite of this winning attitude was called the "Wallenda factor" by Warren Bennis and Burt Nanus in their excellent book, *Leaders: The Strategies for Taking Charge*. They described an occasion when the normally positive-thinking Karl Wallenda, the great high-wire aerialist, engaged in some negative thinking that may have contributed to his death. His task was to walk across a wire that was stretched seventy-five feet above a San Juan, Puerto Rico, downtown street. Wallenda had accomplished numerous other similar feats, but he seemed to take a very worried, somewhat fearful approach to this challenge. Karl's wife, who was also an aerialist, described what she thinks happened:

> All Karl thought about for three straight months prior to [the event] was falling. It was the first time he'd ever thought about that, and it seemed to me that he put all his energies into not falling rather than walking the tightrope.

Mrs. Wallenda added that her husband even went so far as to personally supervise the installation of the tightrope, making certain that the guy wires were secure, "something he had never even thought of doing before" (Bennis and Nanus, p. 70).

The result of Wallenda's effort to accomplish this feat was that his worst fears were realized and he fell to his death. What happened? For the first time, this great aerialist *tried not to fall* instead of just *trying to walk the wire*.

General Brady recounted the same phenomenon from his days as a "Dust-Off" helicopter pilot:

> Imagination is a marvelous thing to have and to figure out the approaches and to do all the things to visualize [success]. But if you also begin to imagine bullets coming through the cockpit or bullets going through your head or dying or burning or any of those things that could happen to you—if you can't turn your imagination away from those things—you're dead!

The application of the Wallenda factor to everyday living has tremendous relevance for both leaders and followers. Have you ever observed people who were trying not to fall rather than trying to walk. Trying not to miss a critical free throw in basketball is very different than just trying to swish the net. Trying not to lose a key customer is different than just trying to satisfy the customer's needs. There are countless applications, but the point remains the same: A positive, can-do attitude is much more likely to lead to success than an attitude that focuses on what could go wrong.

Courage That Defeats Fear

It takes a positive, winning attitude for any of us to achieve our potential. From our observations of these great teams, we have decided that courage is an important dimension of a winning attitude. Nowhere was the presence of this dimension more apparent than when we visited with General Patrick Henry Brady at the Presidio in San Francisco. During the Vietnam conflict, Brady was awarded the nation's highest recognition for combat soldiers, the Medal of Honor, for his courageous helicopter rescues as a "Dust-Off" pilot in a medical evacuation unit. The description of the day that was the focus of the award reads like a chapter from a war novel. But it's not fiction—it really happened. The text of General Brady's Medal of Honor citation is as follows:

> For conspicuous gallantry and intrepidity in action at the risk of his life above and beyond the call of duty. Maj. Brady distinguished himself while serving in the Republic of Vietnam commanding a UH-1H ambulance helicopter, volunteered to rescue wounded men from a site in enemy-held territory which was reported to be heavily defended and to be blanketed

by fog. To reach the site he descended through heavy fog and smoke and hovered slowly along a valley trail, turning his ship sideward to blow away the fog with the backwash from his rotor blades. Despite the unchallenged, close-range enemy fire, he found the dangerously small site, where he successfully landed and evacuated two badly wounded South Vietnamese soldiers. He was then called to another area completely covered by dense fog where American casualties lay only 50 meters from the enemy. Two aircraft had previously been shot down and others had made unsuccessful attempts to reach this site earlier in the day. With unmatched skill and extraordinary courage, Maj. Brady made four flights to this embattled landing zone and successfully rescued all the wounded. On his third mission of the day Maj. Brady once again landed at a site surrounded by the enemy. The friendly ground force, pinned down by enemy fire, had been unable to reach and secure the landing zone. Although his aircraft had been badly damaged and his controls partially shot away during his initial entry into this area, he returned minutes later and rescued the remaining injured. Shortly thereafter, obtaining a replacement aircraft, Maj. Brady was requested to land in an enemy mine field where a platoon of American soldiers was trapped. A mine detonated near his helicopter, wounding two crew members and damaging his ship. In spite of this, he managed to fly six severely injured patients to medical aid. Throughout that day Maj. Brady utilized three helicopters to evacuate a total of 51 seriously wounded men, many of whom would have perished without prompt medical treatment. Maj. Brady's bravery was in the highest traditions of the military service and reflects great credit upon himself and the U.S. Army.

As incredible as this day was, General Brady reports that the day's events were not that unusual for him or other "Dust-Off" pilots:

Well, you know, I had worse days than that. I went through four aircraft on another day. If on that particular day somebody hadn't written that all up and made a fuss about it, I never would have remembered that day any more than others. Too many days were worse—every Dust-Off pilot had them.

What impressed us most about General Brady and his team was their tremendous sense of courage. In reflecting on the character of the twelve real dream team leaders, courage emerges as an overpowering dimension of these people and their teams. The kind of courage that defeats fear seems to be one of those watershed traits that serves to distinguish pretty good team performance from championship performance. We asked General Brady how he was able to overcome fear in such a routinely dangerous environment.

> I never experienced fear. Apprehension is the word I always used—apprehensive because I was thinking about so many things at one time and so focused...I didn't allow fear to take hold of me. Terror...will cause to happen the thing that caused it.

Still, the all-important question remains: Where does this kind of fear-defeating courage come from? Brady has remarkable insight to share on this question:

> ...the foundation of courage—whatever these guys had when you're just not sure [you're going to make it], when all the gauges go and you start smelling gas or people are hurt or whatever—the foundation of all that is faith...I don't think you'll find anybody with courage, moral or physical courage, that's repetitive and that's consistent, who isn't also a person who has faith. Faith—it's a belief that there's something beyond that moment and it's something beyond and above yourself. But if you're tied to the moment in life or if you're tied to yourself in life, you're never going

to be a person with any courage. You're never going
to be a person who contributes.

What a powerful thought! A winning attitude involves
more than just the hope and expectation of success. It
involves a commitment to a cause or mission you have
accepted as being more important than you. That level of
commitment leads to a willingness to take significant risks
in case success is not realized. In General Brady's case,
the risk was his life and the lives of his crew. In the case
of a parent, it could be the courage to believe in and trust
your teenage son or daughter to keep their word or a
commitment to your family members that they are more
important than you are. In a management setting, it could
mean having the courage to deal honestly and fairly with
a really tough issue such as the need for improved performance from a particular team member.

What we're really asking here is, what happens to a
leader and a team when the going gets really tough? Does
the team have the courage to overcome its fears, or does
it fold in the face of adversity? What explains why one
basketball team that falls behind continues to battle back
and win while another simply gives up and just waits for
the game end? In fact, the same question could be applied to people who face adversity and disappointment.
Why do some make spectacular comebacks while others
resign themselves to being less than they could be and
simply wait for their life to be over?

It seems clear that positive versus negative thinking
is a life versus death choice in the cases of Lt. Colonel
Trent and then-Major Brady. It may be less apparent but
it is no less true that positive versus negative thinking is
a life versus death issue for all of us! Nothing kills human
potential, hope, and the joy of living more quickly than
negative thinking. On the other hand, positive thinking
drives out fear, restores hope and joy to living, and enables people to achieve their potential.

The top three blocks of John Wooden's "Pyramid of Success" provide another perspective and additional insight in answering this question. Wooden defines *confidence* as "respect without fear. It may come from being prepared and keeping all things in proper perspective." He defines the second block, *poise*, as "just being yourself—being at ease in any situation—never fighting yourself." These two blocks of his pyramid, along with the other twelve that support them, lead to the apex of the pyramid—*competitive greatness*. Wooden defines competitive greatness as being "at your best when your best is needed—enjoyment of a difficult challenge." Actually, enjoying a difficult challenge is a far cry from fear and is a clear sign of the presence of a winning attitude in a team.

Change Your Thoughts—Change Your Life

No discussion of the concept of a winning attitude would be complete without including the great work of Dr. Norman Vincent Peale and his remarkable wife and life partner, Ruth Stafford Peale. Dr. Peale's accomplishments include serving as pastor of the Marble Collegiate Church in New York for fifty-two years; creating the Peale Center for Christian Living in Pawling, New York; founding and managing *Guideposts* magazine (with a circulation of over four million, twelfth largest in the United States); and authoring numerous books. His most famous book, *The Power of Positive Thinking*, has sold more than fifteen million copies and has been translated into forty languages. The promotional comment on the cover of the 35th Special Anniversary Edition of the book describes it as "the greatest inspirational best seller of the century [that] offers confidence without fear and a life of enrichment and luminous vitality."

In the preface to the 35th Anniversary Edition, Dr. Peale addresses a frequently asked question: Why did you write this book?

> My answer is that it was written out of personal necessity. As a child I was inordinately shy and shrinking...having what I am sure must have been the most highly developed inferiority complex one could possibly imagine.
>
> I constantly minimized myself, thinking that I lacked ability and brains and would probably never amount to anything. This I glumly told myself. Then I became aware that people were agreeing with me, because it is a fact that others intuitively tend to take you at your own self-evaluation.
>
> ...Then one day a professor really let me have it. "Norman," he asked in a private after-class meeting, "what is the matter with you? Why do you go skulking through life as a scared rabbit? You've got enough brains and innate ability to do something in this world. Haven't you got any faith in God or yourself?"....
>
> I stumbled out of his classroom and down the steps of the college building—angry, tearful, and hopeless. Then I stopped short! I recall the exact spot—the fourth step from the bottom—for a thought had pierced my mind. It hit me like a ton of bricks but was more like a burst of light. It was the exciting, almost incredible thought, "I don't have to be this way any longer."
>
> The son of religious parents (my father was a minister), I had been taught where to turn for help, though up to this point I had failed to do so. So there on that fourth step I asked the Lord to take over my life. I committed myself sincerely to Jesus Christ, believing that what I could not do with myself could be done through the grace of God.
>
> I was not suddenly changed, but from that moment, I started down a new road of thinking. Guided by my parents, I began to read writers like Emerson,

Thoreau, Marcus Aurelius, and others who believed
in the power inherent in the human mind. As I read
and studied, I learned the great truth enunciated so
well by William James, who said, "The greatest discovery of my generation is that a human being can
change his life by changing his attitude of mind." I
was a negative thinker but I knew it was fatal to
remain so. Gradually my thinking became more positive. I had read somewhere a statement ascribed to
an ancient thinker, "Take charge of your thoughts.
You can do what you will with them." So gradually I
built a system of thought for myself, and for myself
alone, for I had to form a new and better thought
pattern to attain victory over myself.

At the time of writing the book I had, of course,
no idea that it would ever become one of the best-
selling books in American history. My only concern
then was, as it is now, that the book would continue
to reach the defeated, the failing, the self-doubtful,
the timorous, and the fearful with the assurance that
positive thinking, or the life of faith, is the true secret
of living....I have tried to show how anyone can trans-
form the pain and struggle of human existence into
victorious, constructive everyday living.

Dr. Peale's formula has formed the basis of the positive thinking movement that continues to be espoused by
the likes of Zig Zigler, Lou Holtz, and numerous others.
The belief that we get what we expect is not just some
"feel good" unproven philosophy of living. In fact, numerous academic research studies have provided scientific
evidence to support the power of positive thinking.

Why, then, do so many people allow negative thinking to dominate their lives? Probably because most people
are taught to think negatively by their parents, the educational system, and the organizations where they work.
The rules and policies in most homes, schools, and work
settings are most often stated in a manner that gives
people a very strong "thou shalt not" tone, with very little

emphasis on the "thou shalt." This inordinate emphasis on the negative tends to limit people and, ultimately, damage their self-esteem.

The spiritual dimension of the positive attitude concept is not to be denied. Most of the dream team leaders expressed a reliance on a power beyond themselves as the source of their overwhelming sense of hope and faith that things will work out. Dr. Peale was a master at helping to create that attitude in people.

When we concluded our interview, we thanked Dr. Peale and Ruth Peale for taking the morning to help us with our work. At that point, Dr. Peale asked if he could lead us in a prayer before we departed. Being people of similar faith to Dr. Peale's, we said sure, that would be great. Dr. Peale then led us in a most eloquent prayer in which he asked God to bless "our most important work of sharing ideas that have the potential to help people lead richer and more productive lives." He went on to ask God to give us the insight, persistence, and commitment to see this project through and to write this book. His was not a short prayer. As he continued, we felt our motivation and sense of urgency growing. By the time he concluded, we had raised our aspirations and expectations to a new height.

We thanked him for his prayer for us, which was truly special, but then we had to tell him he had made one pretty critical mistake during his prayer. "You told God that we were writing a book. We didn't want anyone to know just in case we were unsuccessful—now He knows." With a sly grin, Dr. Peale replied, "Well, it looks as if you're just going to have to do it now!"

One woman talked about how her mother had instilled in her the kind of positive self-esteem that leads to a winning attitude. She said that when she was a little girl, her mother would walk out with her each morning to meet the bus. As they heard the bus approaching, her mother would give her a big hug and say, "Helen, you're the most beautiful little girl in the world," and send her on her way to school. Helen said that she was in junior high school before she found out that she was ugly, and then it was too late! If you could meet her today, we think you would agree that she is a most beautiful person, and the distinguishing aspect of her beauty is in her behavior—her smile, her expressiveness, her poise and confidence. She became beautiful as a response to the expectations of her mother.

Carl Joseph is our favorite athlete. In high school, Carl was captain of the basketball team, high-jumped 5'10", and played middle linebacker on the football team. After high school, he went on to become a star middle linebacker for Bethune-Cookman College in Florida. We saw a videotape of Carl leading his high school basketball team on a fast break that resulted in him slam dunking the basketball. So what's the big deal? Well, Carl Joseph only has one leg, and when he plays sports, he doesn't use an artificial leg. Here's a guy with one leg who was a very tough middle linebacker for one of the best small/medium-sized university football programs in the country. The obvious question is one that he has been asked on several occasions: Don't you know that people with just one leg don't do things like this? His reply is quick and clear:

> No, I didn't know that when I was young. I grew up out in the country and the only people that I had much contact with were my friends and my family. My mother always told me that I could do anything I wanted to do, so I just went out and did it and my mother and my friends encouraged me. It's really no big deal.

Sorry Carl, but we don't agree. We think it is a really big deal for anyone to realize so much of their potential. We also think it is a really big deal to be surrounded by people like your mother and your friends who created such a positive, expectant environment.

It is interesting to note that the crucial role of instilling a winning attitude in both Helen and Carl was filled by their mothers—people who really care for them. The challenge to parents, teachers, managers, and other leaders is this: Negativism is natural and easy. Do you really care enough about the people you lead to take the time and energy necessary to create a positive environment where people can develop winning attitudes?

FROM SEVEN CONCEPTS TO SEVEN PRACTICES: PUTTING TEAMWORK INTO ACTION

The concepts and stories presented in the preceding chapters are intended to convince you to adopt the teamwork philosophy and to begin seeking practical ways to implement the team approach in your world. This final chapter is designed to stimulate your thinking about the practical "how-to's" for leaders who are sincere in their desire to build real dream teams.

From Concepts To Practices
To Patterns Of Behavior

Like individuals, teams develop behavioral patterns and habits that are revealed through their practices and actions. As reported from the experience of the real dream teams, their success is driven by their practices and not just their intellectual agreement with the concepts. In a business, for example, strategic planning may be done along with total quality management and even team-building activities. But if consistent action built around the seven practices of real dream teams is missing, then the actions and behaviors seem isolated and ineffective and the vision seems non-existent or meaningless. When daily activities do not align with the vision in a meaningful way, the potentially healthy, productive patterns never become practice.

A practice, then, is a norm, a standard, a pattern of behavior that becomes a recognized way of relating and working. Clearly recognized and reinforced patterns become the standards or norms of the team. For those who invest in the team's future, the practices become valued, then accepted, then comfortable, and finally automatic over time.

Change Process

How To Move From Ineffective To Effective		
Phase 1	*Phase 2*	*Phase 3*
Current Ineffective Team Practices	Desired Transitional Team Practices	Highly Effective Team Practices
Unconscious	Conscious	Unconscious
Automatic	Deliberate	Automatic
Comfortable	Uncomfortable	Comfortable
Ineffective	Effective	Highly Effective

Changing team practices and moving toward greater effectiveness has to be a conscious and deliberate process. We find that current team practices, old habits if you will, are often so accepted and outside the team's awareness that they remain unchallenged. A long-term commitment and a belief in the process is required to sustain the effort.

In addition, teams must accept from the beginning that getting to phase 3, where new practices become automatic, comfortable, and effective, means going through the transitional phase 2. To gain the benefits of new patterns and practices, every team must experience the discomfort of transition. Awkwardness and uncomfortableness, those predictable ingredients of change, will indeed be a part of the remedy for ailing teams that choose to get better.

The seven practices provide the process for working together to reach the future. The process must be chosen, it must be shared by the stakeholders, and it must be the new template against which team effectiveness is measured.

The Fabric Of Teamwork

As discussed in the introduction, the seven practices can be viewed as the "threads that comprise the fabric of teamwork." This view of the practices helps to emphasize the need to view all seven practices as being necessary for real dream team experiences. If one thread is missing or torn, then the fabric unravels. A team may be very good at most of the practices, but the lack of attention to one or two practices negates the effectiveness of the others.

While we believe the seven practices can be successfully applied to any team setting, we don't pretend to be able to tell you the specifics of how you should apply them to your team. If you're convinced that adopting a team leadership style is the right thing to do, then we're convinced you will be able to combine the ideas outlined in this book, your knowledge of your team and its activities, and the ideas from the resources we suggest in this chapter to make your team more effective. To stimulate your thinking, we have compiled a series of ideas/suggestions to facilitate the development of each of the seven practices in your team.

Developing Practices

To make the transition from the dream team concept to real dream team practices, visualize the change process model. During the transition from concept to practice, you are choosing *conscious* and *deliberate* strategies for making each of the seven practices so much a part of your fabric that they become unconscious, automatic, comfortable, and acceptable. Therefore, you and your team must make a long-term commitment to the development of the seven practices.

Practice #1: Owning The Mission

1. In opening this chapter, we suggested that extraordinary results begin with somebody's dream and that the dream must be shared and embraced by the team members. Every indicator from our research and involvement with numerous teams points to this practice as the most necessary and essential practice of real dream teams.

Therefore, your organization, your team, your family, or your group must begin with a shared vision of the future. As Stephen Covey suggests in his book on highly effective individuals, "Begin with the end in mind." Establish first with your team the shared belief or assumption that you can only be truly effective when you all pull in the same direction. If the direction is wrong or people have different views of the future and the mission, the very best intentions and efforts will counteract each other. The members of your team will be in an unintentional but fatal tug of war with each other.

Therefore, you must develop with your team the common mental model that sharing a mission is absolutely essential to your success.

2. Devote significant time to a strategy for clarifying your view of the future and your mission. For organizations, we highly recommend Hamel and Prahalad's *Competing for the Future.* These authors add helpful clarity to the concept that you and your organization will be somewhere in five years, so why not create, control, and shape where you will be? You do have a choice, don't you? A choice between reactive and proactive, between passive and assertive, and between victim and creator of circumstances.

If you don't have a healthy strategic planning process, put one in place. The goal is to develop a common view of the future five to ten years out, a mission to lead you on your pathway to the future, and some clear short-term tactical goals that support the mission.

3. Develop your strategy and mission with the involvement of all your people. Since the mark of a solid mission is the ownership, commitment, and excitement of the total team, involve the people who must implement the mission in a way to assure their excitement, commitment, and passion. In short, people give their best if they believe in what they do. If they do not, they "put in their time" in order to get to the weekend, when they can do things about which they really feel passionately.

4. Develop your plan with enough detail that you will be able to measure progress toward the vision and mission. If we are progressing toward our mission in six months, one year, two years, and beyond:

- How will our organization look different?
- What processes will be different?

- How will people act and what will people do differently?

- Who will be new partners and on whom will we have dependencies?

- What new competencies must we develop?

- What new learning tools and processes will help our people think together more effectively and add speed to our overall efforts?

- How will we be aligned throughout our organization or team to be better connected to our mission?

5. Tell the mission story over and over and over. Create opportunities to connect daily activities to core values and mission. Your mission is the mission if you are team leader.

6. The litmus test is to ask a representative sample of people from your team what the mission is, why it is important, and what must be done well (strengths, competencies) if you are to be successful. What you hear will tell you how well your attempt to create a mission-driven team is working.

Practice #2: Mutual Support, Respect, And Encouragement

1. Establish with your team or teams the idea that building trust through mutual support, respect, and encouragement is a shared value. Teams must first operate from a common belief before they will change their external behavior. Talk openly and honestly about trust, establishing and building trust, and how you can only achieve the results all of you want if a climate of trust exists. Relate this to opening the "arena" of shared information presented in the chapter on empowering communication.

2. Solicit honest feedback, either verbal or written, about the level of trust in your team. Ask yourself if the selected feedback tool solicits honest and meaningful information. Remember that the system has not traditionally rewarded honest feedback *to* team leaders. The messenger has often been shot! Be careful how you solicit this feedback, because most people don't really trust team leaders initially. We know you mean well, but trust us—team leaders overestimate the trust level of a group.

3. Ask your team members to rate their trust with each other and you on a scale of 1 (low) to 10 (high). Ask them to explain their ratings in writing. Then ask them to indicate specific actions that could be taken to increase trust, support, and respect within the team.

4. Design activities that allow the team to work together toward clearly defined goals. Success is reaching the team goal, not individual goals. Activities could range from a desired independent work objective to an outdoor experiential "challenge" course similar to the one routinely used by the folks at Saturn Automotive. To develop trust, respect, support, and encouragement, there must be common objectives and common incentives. If it is impossible to reach the goal without a new degree of risking and trusting, and if the risking and trusting are rewarded, new behaviors will occur.

Practice #3: Role Clarification And Negotiation

1. Connect each person's role to the mission. Each person really does make a difference. Clarifying each person's role and connecting it to the mission allows each person to truly believe that his or her work makes a difference.

After completing the team mission or after challenging the mission, invite each team member to write down and then verbalize how his or her role contributes to the mission and the team.

2. Next, clarify each person's perception of his or her role and responsibilities. Discuss these perceptions openly within the team.

3. Now use the role clarification and negotiation strategy discussed in the chapter on roles. This procedure is consistently successful and helpful in our teaming sessions. One-on-one role negotiations should be used between all people who have dependencies on each other. In effect, it is a role enhancement opportunity for each person to understand how their behavior impacts others, both positively and negatively, and to learn what others want that could contribute to their effectiveness.

4. Consider using the "Personnel Relations Survey" available through Teleometrics with a resulting Johari Window profile to prepare for role negotiations. It works! Listening—real listening—and honest information sharing about ways to increase job effectiveness is a high-payoff activity.

Mastering Practice #1, shared mission, and Practice #3, clarifying and negotiating roles, will quickly improve team functioning. People are highly motivated by the knowledge of how to win together through a common mission and shared objectives. They are equally motivated when they establish a "line of sight" between their daily work and the mission.

Practice #4: Win–Win Cooperation

1. Talk with your team about traditional American competition (win–lose) and the new collaborative, synergistic team approach called win–win. Better yet, have them experience the approaches in a simulation exercise.

2. Identify potential win–lose situations that currently exist within your team, between teams, or in your organization. Remember that a win–lose situation occurs when one person or team wins at the expense of another, regardless of the good intentions of the winner. Typical win–lose deals include incentive systems that reward one organizational team for success at the expense of the organization, school athletic programs that win at the expense of academic programs, a system that allows men to consistently win key management positions at the expense of talented women, and individual stars who are allowed to win at the expense of the team.

3. Reward collaborative efforts and eliminate *anything* that makes it acceptable to win at someone else's expense. People do what the system rewards. No amount of team building will help if the infrastructure does not support teamwork effort.

4. Make heroes of collaborators, those who improve the process of working together toward common objectives.

Practice #5: Building Technical, Personal, And Teaming Competencies

1. In the new environment described in the introduction, external change forces of revolutionary proportion could overwhelm the discovery of your team's pathway to the future. Since you don't control either the forces of environmental change or your competition, we suggest you seize the controllable variable, *your response.* View your response, namely the ability to learn together as a team and the ability to speed the learning process with recognized learning tools, as a distinct competitive advantage. Those who learn fastest get the prize.

Commit collectively to learning how to learn together. Assess your learning competencies in three key areas: technical, personal, and team. Think of them as "core learning competencies." In a team environment, technical knowledge, even individual brilliance, is diminished without the ability to articulate and share with teammates.

2. Adding value to the team will be the job security of the future. Job enrichment and adding value will become synonymous with security. Tenure, seniority, and technical competence alone will no longer be enough.

3. We have three suggestions for technical enhancement. First, benchmark against a best-practices model. What do people do when they are at their best? Second, go directly to your people. What do they believe they need to do their jobs more effectively? Third, consider adopting concepts such as "knowledge units" and "pay for versatility," like our friends at Post Cereals.

4. For personal enhancement, we suggest the "personal mastery" tools from Innovation Associates and the learning tools associated with Stephen Covey's group.

5. For team enhancement, we suggest the work of Kimball Fisher, particularly *Leading Self-Directed Work Teams*, and team learning opportunities available through consulting groups.

Your investment in building core learning competencies is indeed a serious and long-term commitment. It simply means you really do believe people are your most important asset.

Practice #6: Empowering Communication

1. Clearly identify what your team has the power to make happen. Kimball Fisher, a leading authority on self-directed work teams, suggests the following empowerment equation: *Empowerment = f(Authority, Resources, Information, Accountability)*. If any of the four variables goes to zero, empowerment goes to zero.

Effective teams have the power to get things done because the new team norms empower people to play their roles to the hilt (authority) and enjoy the rewards and disappointments of their effort (accountability). Empowering communication is the tool that encourages clear understanding about authority, accountability, and necessary resources and information.

For what does your team have authority, responsibility, and accountability? A clear understanding of these issues sets the parameters for empowerment. If there are boundaries and guidelines, clarify them here. The boundaries for Team Taurus were to build a medium-size car that would sell in the $17,500 to $21,000 price range and stay within the project budget. Empowerment is the ability of the team to, as Jean-Luc Picard of "Star Trek" fame might say, "Make it so!" Therefore, identify what your team can absolutely make happen, put their arms around, and say, "This is ours."

2. The Johari Window concept presented earlier is one learning concept around which your team can develop more open communication. Very useful self as well as team effectiveness inventories are available through Teleometrics, Inc., at reasonable cost. The resulting profiles clearly show the size of each person's arena, blind spot, facade, and unutilized potential windows. This tool can provide a shared understanding and dialogue for deliberate acknowledgment of communication and information needs as well as team roadblocks to greater effectiveness.

Also, consider the above learning tool as a prerequisite to role clarification and negotiation.

3. Consider a communication–learning coach or facilitator. The emerging collection of knowledge and the successful application of learning disciplines are valuable resources to speed individual, team, and organizational learning. In *The Fifth Discipline* and *The Fifth Discipline Fieldbook*, readers will find practical tools for visioning, systems thinking, personal mastery, challenging current mental models, and learning to communicate more effectively as a team. As author Peter Senge admonishes, think about communicating and learning faster than the competition as a sustainable source of competitive advantage. Whether or not you are in a competitive situation, being able to consistently and non-defensively discuss assumptions underlying decisions and strategies is a productive practice for any team, from the National Security Council to the local Rotary Club to your family.

A coach or facilitator can help you and your team get started in learning how to learn together. Such an individual can rapidly speed the learning curve and could prove to be a wise investment.

Practice #7: Winning Attitude

1. Remember Lou Holtz's "we're not leaving this room until each person comes up with one reason we can win this ball game" approach? Your people, your team members, your committee, or your family has to first believe they can win (reach the mission). Of course, the key is that you all define winning and why, together, you can win.

Craft a statement together that specifically states why you believe your team can be successful. In fact, connect this directly to your vision, mission, and statement of values. If you don't believe you can reach your mission, then the mission is meaningless.

2. Select a learning resource and a teaching resource, if possible. Since the practice of winning attitude has to be conscious and deliberate, we again suggest Peter Senge's collection of works in the *Fifth Discipline* and *The Fifth Discipline Fieldbook*, particularly focusing on mental models and team learning. The goal is helping your team talk to each other in helpful ways and challenging those silent assumptions that are self-defeating and limiting.

For your own motivation and impetus to begin this practice, read *The Power of Positive Thinking* by Norman Vincent Peale.

3. Model the way. One of the new roles of leadership is helping others believe in the vision and believe in themselves.

4. Bust paradigms. Lead the way in sharing the victories that come from thinking differently. Publish stories of individuals and teams that got "out of the box" of old thinking habits and allowed themselves to approach challenges differently. "Think globally, act locally" is not only relevant for protection of the environment but also a healthy reminder for all to find new ways of seeing things. In the fullest sense, we are limited only by our vision.

Examples Of Teams That Work

Our experience with team development began almost fifteen years ago with for the Kimberly-Clark Corporation facilities in Conway, Arkansas; Memphis, Tennessee; Beech Island, South Carolina; and Marquette, Michigan. Since then, we have worked with a wide variety of organizations to help them build the seven practices of real dream teams into their operations. These organizations have ranged from large and small businesses to hospitals, government agencies, churches, families, and community organizations. The organizational philosophies involved have ranged from radically self-directed teams to traditional authority-based organizations.

Although the specific applications differed in each situation, all of the organizations benefited from examining how they can more effectively implement the seven practices. In fact, our confidence in the practices has been strengthened through our work with Arkla Gas, Alltel Information Services, Tyson Foods, the City of Fayetteville, the City of Hot Springs, the City of Booneville, Reynolds Metals Company, Carrier Air Conditioning, Acxiom, Post Cereals, Best Foods, Maybelline Corporation, Falcon Jet, and over 250 other organizations.

The self-directed team system at Best Foods (a division of CPC International) in Little Rock, Arkansas, is the most radical we have found. This system was implemented when the plant, which produces Skippy Peanut Butter, was opened in 1978. Based on ideas conceptualized by Lou Davis, their UCLA professor/consultant, the plant has *no* supervisors and a very small core management staff. The empowering rationale of Davis's design was to take the various roles that have been traditionally performed by supervisors and distribute them to the workers. For example, one role traditionally performed by supervisors is to check attendance. In the Best Foods system, the responsibility for monitoring attendance belongs to one of the operations workers. Another typical supervisory role is to make work assignments, which is assigned to another worker, and so forth. Each worker is assigned a "supervisory" role and the roles are rotated over time.

The system also provides for separate teams of workers to set the norms for the operations, administer the training/certification program, and make judgments about adherence to norms. The core management team can make decisions to override team decisions, but when this happens it is recognized as the worst possible outcome and prompts discussions about how to improve the system. To show how "leading edge" the Best/Davis system is, in 1978 they named the system "A Search for a Better Way to Manage." Long before the buzzword continuous improvement flowed from the total quality management movement, a basic tenant of the Best/Davis system acknowledged that their management process should be continuously evaluated and improved.

Does self-management work? At Best Foods, the results speak for themselves, as the plant has become the company's star facility. The Kraft-General Foods Post Cereals-Jonesboro operation has achieved spectacular results that have drawn attention throughout the Post and parent Kraft Foods family. The Reynolds Gum Springs plant has achieved a level of union/management cooperation through teamwork that has exceeded what many thought was possible. From Fortune 50 companies to families, from volunteer to private groups, from athletic to community teams, we have seen extraordinary results achieved by using the seven practices.

The New Environment And Team Strategy Connection

We have made a case around the inextricable connection between the demands of the new environment and the superior nature of responses available through teaming strategies. The evolutionary change required by the challenges of the new environment signals fundamental new imperatives:

- This is a revolution. We must stick together in order to win.

- Change is scary and often chaotic. We must learn together how to embrace change and create comfort from chaos.

- We must share a vision and a passion for the future.

- Stretching to reach the future vision requires the best thinking, best collaborative effort, and highest commitment of every person on the team.

- We can only get to the future together. Win–win philosophies will prevail.

- Future vision and daily thoughts, feelings, and actions must be in harmony for ultimate success.

- Bold strategic initiatives, reengineering, reorganization, and total quality management will succeed only to the degree that internal systems and processes support the future vision and only to the degree that people team together to reach the vision.

- Teaming success will be yours if you and your team are conscious, deliberate, and committed to making the seven practices a way of life.

Your Search For A Better Way

If you have stayed with this book to this point, you obviously are interested in a better way. We hope this book has stirred the very core of your motivational driving forces. All of us do want more for ourselves, our families, and the other teams to which we are committed.

We have seen and experienced a better way. It is not the only way, but we know the seven practices are powerful and empowering. If you are willing to make a genuine commitment to the seven practices, you can build a real dream team of your own. The seven practices help create an environment where people can truly give their best effort. The practices are freeing and unleash individual and team potential. Most of all, the practices of real dream teams allow people to connect to their deepest inner needs: to be a part of something beyond themselves and to make a difference in this world.

Pathway To The Future In The Revolutionary New Environment

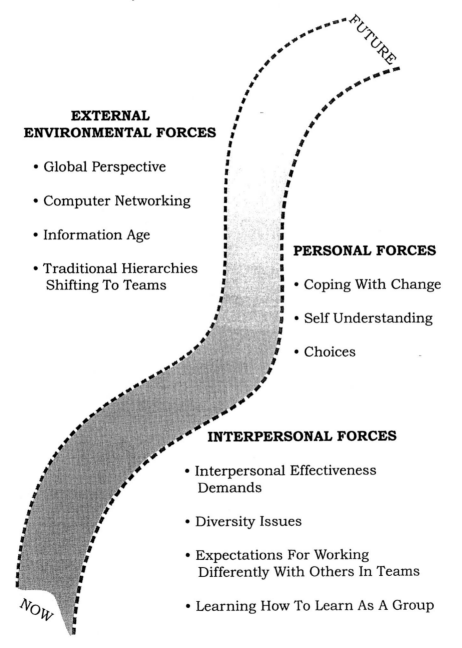

EXTERNAL ENVIRONMENTAL FORCES

- Global Perspective

- Computer Networking

- Information Age

- Traditional Hierarchies Shifting To Teams

PERSONAL FORCES

- Coping With Change

- Self Understanding

- Choices

INTERPERSONAL FORCES

- Interpersonal Effectiveness Demands

- Diversity Issues

- Expectations For Working Differently With Others In Teams

- Learning How To Learn As A Group

FUTURE

NOW

BIBLIOGRAPHY

Bennis, Warren and Burt Nanus. *Leaders: The Strategies for Taking Charge.* New York: Harper and Row, 1985.

Bolton, Robert. *People Skills.* New York: Touchstone/Simon and Shuster, 1979.

Covey, Stephen F. *The Seven Habits of Highly Effective People.* New York: Simon and Shuster, 1989.

Drucker, Peter. *Management: Tasks, Responsibilities, Practices.* New York: Harper and Row, 1973.

Fayol, Henry. *General and Industrial Management* (revised by Irwin Gray). Belmont, CA: David S. Lake Publishers, 1987.

Fisher, Kimball. *Leading Self-Directed Work Teams.* New York: McGraw-Hill, 1993.

Gardner, John William. *On Leadership.* New York: Free Press, 1990.

Hamel, Gary and C.K. Prahalad. *Competing for the Future.* Boston: Harvard Business Press. 1994.

Kanter, Rosabeth Moss. *The Change Masters.* New York: Simon and Shuster, 1983.

Naisbitt, John and Patricia Aburdene. *Re-Inventing the Corporation: Transforming Your Job and Your Company for the New Information Society.* New York: Warner Books, 1985.

Naisbitt, John and Patricia Aburdene. *Megatrends 2000: The New Directions for the 1990s.* New York: Morrow, 1990.

Peale, Norman Vincent. *The Power of Positive Thinking.* New York: Prentice-Hall, 1952.

Peters, Thomas J. *Thriving on Chaos: Handbook for a Management Revolution* (First edition). New York: Knopf, 1987.

Peters, Thomas J. and Robert H. Waterman, Jr. *In Search of Excellence.* New York: Harper and Row, 1982.

Ringer, Robert J. *Winning Through Intimidation.* Los Angeles: Los Angeles Book Publishers Company, 1974.

Ringer, Robert J. *Looking Out for Number One.* Beverly Hills, CA: Los Angeles Book Corporation, 1977.

Schuller, Robert. *Tough Times Never Last, But Tough People Do!* Nashville: T. Nelson Publishers, 1983.

Senge, Peter M. *The Fifth Discipline: The Art and Practice of Learning Organizations.* New York: Currency Doubleday, 1990.

Senge, Peter M., Charlotte Roberts, Richard B. Ross, Bryan J. Smith, and Art Kleiner. *The Fifth Discipline Fieldbook.* New York: Doubleday, 1994.

Teleometrics International, The Woodlands, Texas.

The Living Bible. Wheaton, IL: Tyndal House Publishing, 1971.

Tichy, Noel M. and Stratford Sherman. *Control Your Destiny or Someone Else Will.* New York: Doubleday, 1993.

Toffler, Alvin. *Future Shock.* New York: Random House, 1970.

Toffler, Alvin. *The Third Wave* (First edition). New York: Morrow, 1980.

If you have a dream team experience you would like to share with the authors, you can contact them at:

Robert Fisher, Ph.D.
Vice President for Academic Affairs
Arkansas State University
P.O. Box 179
State University, AR 72467
Phone: 501-972-2030
Fax: 501-972-2036
Internet: rfisher@omaha.astate.edu

Bo Thomas, Ph.D.
The Thomas Consulting Group
10809 Executive Center Drive
Suite 115
Little Rock, AR 72211
Phone: 501-223-9991